LUDWIG
BEETHOVEN

CLASSIC *f*M LIFELINES

LUDWIG VAN BEETHOVEN

AN ESSENTIAL GUIDE TO HIS LIFE AND WORKS

STEPHEN JOHNSON

PAVILION

First published in Great Britain in 1997 by
PAVILION BOOKS LIMITED
26 Upper Ground, London SE1 9PD

Edited and designed by Castle House Press, Penarth, South Wales
Cover designed by Bet Ayer

A CIP catalogue record for this book is available
from the British Library

ISBN 1 86205 001 5

Set in Lydian and Caslon
Printed and bound in Great Britain by Mackays of Chatham

2 4 6 8 10 9 7 5 3 1

This book can be ordered direct from the publisher.
Please contact the Marketing Department.
But try your bookshop first.

ACKNOWLEDGMENTS

To list all the people who have made instructive remarks or helpful suggestions on the subject of Beethoven would be impossible, but some have to be singled out. My thanks, first, to the composer Robert Simpson for giving me (possibly without realizing it) several valuable informal tutorials on Beethoven's music. Thanks also to professors Alexander Goehr, Brian Newbould and Ian Kemp for challenging received ideas and suggesting new, less convention-bound ways of approaching and discussing the music. Recording and writing up interviews for *Gramophone* and *The Independent* offered another, often very entertaining means of continuing my musical education – and the opportunity to discuss Beethoven with the likes of the conductors Gunter Wand, John Eliot Gardiner, Sir Colin Davies, Sir Charles Mackerras and Roger Norrington, the pianist Stephen Kovacevic, and the leader of the Lindsay Quartet, Peter Cropper. Unfortunately, I have never met Charles Rosen, author of *The Classical Style*, but the influence of his writing on my own understanding of Haydn, Mozart and Beethoven has been considerable, and the debt of gratitude I feel to him is almost personal. I also thank my friend Rüdiger Gorner, editor of a valuable short collection of Beethoven's letters, for his help in understanding the German language of Beethoven's time, and his own, idiosyncratic use of it.

But I should end with a special acknowledgment to those in my immediate family who ensured that Beethoven was part of my life for as long as I can remember: my grandfather, Irvine Willis Johnson, and my parents, to whom this book is gratefully dedicated.

Contents

A NOTE FROM THE EDITORS

A biography of this type inevitably contains numerous references to pieces of music. The paragraphs are also peppered with 'quotation marks', since much of the tale is told through reported speech.

Because of this, and to make things more accessible for the reader as well as easier on the eye, we decided to simplify the method of typesetting the names of musical works. Conventionally this is determined by the nature of the individual work, following a set of rules whereby some pieces appear in italics, some in italics and quotation marks, others in plain roman type and others still in roman and quotation marks.

In this book, the names of all musical works are simply set in italics. Songs and arias appear in italics and quotation marks.

CHAPTER 1

BACKGROUND AND BEGINNINGS

(1770–92)

- ♦ Beethoven's lineage
- ♦ An early talent
- ♦ Fascination with Mozart
- ♦ First meeting with Haydn

There is an old and subtle Chinese curse – 'May you live in interesting times.' Ludwig van Beethoven lived in very interesting times. From our safe vantage point in the late twentieth century, the events he would have seen or heard about make exciting reading. But to many continental Europeans who lived through this period of international upheaval and epoch-making social change, the world must have seemed an uncomfortable, if not, at times, a downright terrifying place.

If this sounds like exaggeration, consider some of the more important happenings of Beethoven's lifetime. At the time of his birth in December 1770, much of the German-speaking world was joined in a loose confederacy of states, centred on Austria's Catholic Habsburg monarchy, under the grand although somewhat misleading title of the Holy Roman Empire. Aristocratic values prevailed, and even a composer of the stature of Haydn could still be, in effect, a liveried servant.

By the time of Beethoven's death in 1827, the Holy Roman Empire had ceased to exist, the aristocracy had conceded much of its power to an increasingly influential bourgeoisie, and the image of the composer had been transformed into that of the romantic hero.

Between those two dates had come the French Revolution, the beheading of the French king Louis XVI, the Napoleonic Wars, and the redrawing of the map of Europe, first by Napoleon Bonaparte and then, at the Congress of Vienna, by representatives of all the major European powers.

Of course, challenges to the old order had been reverberating for some time before Beethoven's birth. The eighteenth century had long been labelled the age of 'the Enlightenment', during which the ideas of Voltaire and Jean-Jacques Rousseau in France, and Isaac Newton, John Locke and David Hume in Britain, were a source of nervousness in high places. In most respects, however, the city in which Beethoven was born, Bonn, remained committed to the old order. It was the capital of an old-fashioned church-state, the seat of the Archbishop Elector of Cologne, Maximilian Friedrich, who apparently showed more interest in music, art and architecture than in the wretched conditions of his poorer subjects.

An English traveller, arriving at Bonn by river in 1765, noted how the palace 'makes a fine figure from the water, having a most extensive front', and contrasted it with the 'narrow and ill-built' streets. The aim of many a talented musician was an appointment at the electoral court, and this is what Beethoven's grandfather, also named Ludwig van Beethoven, had achieved in 1733, at the age of twenty-one.

The older Ludwig was of Flemish birth, the son of an ambitious master baker from the town of Malines (or Mechelen). A man of strong principles and fine musicianship, he had risen to achieve the rank of court *Kapellmeister* (director of music) in 1761. The young Ludwig always remembered him with pride and affection, even though he was only three years old when the elder Ludwig died.

Beethoven's father, Johann van Beethoven, was another matter entirely. Although he, too, was musically gifted enough to be chosen for court employment, he was highly unstable, with a growing dependency on drink. His marriage to a young, socially inferior widow, Maria Magdalena Leym, née Keverich (daughter of a kitchen overseer at the palace of Ehrenbreitstein) displeased Ludwig senior, but this patient, quiet, intelligent and well-organized woman seems to have won the old man round, and for the young Ludwig she was always a valuable counterbalance to the volatile Johann: 'a good, kind mother to me, and indeed my best friend', was how he remembered her in later life. She bore Johann seven children, although only three – Ludwig, and his brothers Caspar Carl and Nikolaus Johann – survived into adulthood.

This, then, was Beethoven's lineage. Rumours, however, were soon to grow up about his 'real' background. It was suggested, for instance, that he might have had Spanish blood – not quite as unlikely as it might initially seem: Belgium had remained under Spanish domination until the Treaty of Utrecht in 1713. In the mind of some, Beethoven's black hair, swarthy looks and fiery temperament appeared as a confirmation of this, and the fact that his final address was the *Schwarzspanierhaus* ('Black Spaniard House') added a kind of mystical seal. Another story that went into circulation in Beethoven's lifetime was that he was, in fact, the natural son of Friedrich Wilhelm II, the King of Prussia. Beethoven does not seem to have gone out of his way to contradict this story, despite its improbability, and even despite the obvious slur on the good name of his supposedly beloved mother.

Perhaps Beethoven welcomed the excuse to cast doubts on his own paternity. His feelings towards his father were far from affectionate, which, given Johann's behaviour, is hardly surprising. There are horrible accounts of the four- or five-year-old Ludwig being dragged to the keyboard or the violin, sometimes late at night, and of his being severely beaten or locked in the cellar for the slightest misdemeanour. One childhood friend, Cäcilia Fischer, remembered seeing him standing, weeping, on a little footstool in front of the piano while his father bullied and blustered.

Johann had at least recognized his son's remarkable talent, but it seems he was driven at least partly by thoughts of glory and financial reward of having an infant prodigy in the family – tales of the dazzling successes of the young Mozart would still have been much in circulation. And perhaps Johann hoped that his son would succeed where he had failed. His application for the post of *Kapellmeister*, when old Ludwig died in 1773, had been turned down, and it was soon after that that his drink problem became significantly worse.

Given such an upbringing it is surprising that Beethoven was not put off music for life. In fact, his talents blossomed. In 1778, at the age of seven, he gave what was probably his first public concert, in Cologne. It doesn't seem to have made any great impact at the time, although one or two discerning people were beginning to notice the young musician.

Then, in 1779, came a stroke of luck. The composer Christian Gottlob Neefe arrived in Bonn and took up the post of court organist. Before long Beethoven was studying with him, a real teacher at last, and one who quickly recognized his pupil's outstanding abilities.

Neefe was a very different kind of man from Johann van Beethoven. He was cultivated, well-read in literature and philosophy and, like Beethoven's grandfather, a man of principle and an excellent all-round musician. Neefe was also – unusually for the time – an enthusiast for the music of J.S. Bach. Under his guidance, Beethoven tackled and mastered the great keyboard collection *The Well-tempered Klavier* (which was then available only in handwritten copies) – an experience for which he was to be deeply grateful in later life.

It was after he began studying with Neefe that Beethoven started to compose seriously. His first surviving piece, a set of keyboard variations on a march by Ernst Christoph Dressler, WoO 63 [*Werk ohne Opuszahl* = work without opus number], appeared in 1782. Interestingly, the key of Dressler's march, and therefore of Beethoven's variations – C minor – is one that was to have great significance for the adult composer. This was the key he chose for monumental tragic-heroic works like the *Third Piano Concerto* Op.37, the '*Pathétique*' *Sonata* Op.13 No.8, the first movement of the final *Piano Sonata* Op.111 No.32, the '*Coriolan*' *Overture* Op.62 and, most famously of all, the *Fifth Symphony* Op.67. There, however, similarities between the *Dressler Variations* and the mature Beethoven end.

Under Neefe's supervision, Beethoven was soon trying longer works. The three so-called '*Kurfürsten*' *Piano Sonatas* WoO 47, appeared the following year, in 1783. At about the same time, a notice appeared in the journal *Magazin der Musik*:

Ludwig van Beethoven, son of the above-mentioned tenor, is an eleven-year-old boy [sic] of very promising talent. He plays on the piano in a very finished manner and with power, reads at sight and, to put it briefly, plays the better part of the

Well-tempered Clavier *of Sebastian Bach which Herr Neefe gave him. . . . [Neefe] is now teaching him composition and in order to encourage him, has had engraved in Mannheim 9 Variations on a March. This young genius deserves a subsidy in order to enable him to travel. He will undoubtably become a second Mozart, if he continues as well as he has begun.*

It was also at about this time that Beethoven got to know two people who were to be important to him throughout his life – although to be close to Beethoven could be something of a mixed blessing.

The first, Stephan von Breuning, was a little younger than Ludwig, and a member of a prominent Bonn family. The von Breuning house, where the teenage Beethoven was a frequent visitor, was praised by another guest for its 'unforced atmosphere of culture' and its 'abundance of youthful high spirits'. Beethoven, he wrote, was 'treated as one of the children of the family, and he spent not only the greatest part of the day there, but even many nights'.

The writer was a young medical student, Franz Wegeler – the other lifelong friend Beethoven made at this time. Wegeler left several written recollections of the composer, which are valuable because, unlike many who wrote of their memories of Beethoven, he seems to have had little interest in elaboration or myth-making.

Wegeler and others have left a vivid portrait of the young composer. He was receptive, enquiring, but not a natural student. At school – which he left at eleven – he failed to distinguish himself academically, and in later life gaps showed in his education – his mathematics, for instance, could be surprisingly shaky. Outside school he was solitary, ill-groomed, often pensive, sometimes surly. He was at his happiest when wandering the countryside, contemplating the Rhine or the distant Sieben Gebirge hills, or perhaps composing in his head as he walked – something he was to do increasingly in later years.

Cäcilia Fischer remembered seeing him staring fixedly out of his bedroom window, his head in his hands. 'What are you looking at, Ludwig?' she called up to him. No answer. Later she tried again: 'What does that mean? No answer is also an answer.' 'Oh no,' came the reply, 'it's not like that. Forgive me. I was so taken up with deep and beautiful thoughts that I just couldn't bear to be disturbed.'

The notice in *Magazin der Musik* had spoken of Beethoven's need to travel. A period of time elapsed before that need was met. In 1784 the old Elector, Maximilian Friedrich, died. He was replaced by Maximilian Franz, brother of the Emperor Joseph II, and ties between Bonn and Vienna were strengthened. Shortly after the arrival of Maximilian Franz, Beethoven was appointed joint court organist, with Neefe, at a good salary. His musical output was growing and becoming more ambitious. A set of three piano quartets appeared in 1785, not long after his first attempt at a piano concerto. But there are signs that Beethoven was beginning to find Bonn too small and provincial, and he must have been delighted when it was announced in 1787 that enough funds had been raised to send him to Vienna, possibly to study with Mozart.

Beethoven left for Vienna in March 1787. He did meet Mozart, and played for him. According to one account, Mozart's first reaction wasn't enthusiastic – 'Very pretty, but studied'. But when Beethoven began to improvise, the older composer began to listen more closely: 'Keep an eye on him', he told the other listeners. 'One day he will give the world something to talk about.' But after only two weeks in Vienna, Beethoven received some shocking news: his mother was dying of consumption.

He hurried back to Bonn in time to watch his mother die on 17 July (she was followed a few months later by her infant daughter Maria Margaretha). Beethoven was grief-struck, but the effect on his father Johann was more devastating still. Deprived of his wife's strong support, and with his musical powers failing, he went to pieces and was eventually forced to resign his post at the court. By 1789 Ludwig, although still in his teens, had become the chief wage-earner and was now effectively the head of the family.

And yet, in spite of all this personal tribulation, Beethoven continued to grow musically. At the beginning of 1789 he joined the court theatre orchestra where, over the next two years, he played the viola in three Mozart operas: *Die Entführung aus dem Serail* (*The abduction from the Seraglio*), *Le nozze di Figaro* (*The marriage of Figaro*) and *Don Giovanni*. This in itself must have been a wonderful musical education.

Then, in February 1790, came the news of the death of the Emperor Joseph II. Joseph was well known as an enlightened and enthusiastic reformer, and the young Beethoven, already a passionate believer in freedom and human rights, had admired him. He had been delighted to catch a glimpse of Joseph during his short visit to Vienna in 1787. In remembrance of him, Beethoven composed a '*Cantata on the death of the Emperor Joseph II*', for soloists, chorus and orchestra. Here the nineteen-year-old composer seems to have found his voice at last. Years later, Brahms was to write that 'if there were no name on the title page, no other could be conjectured – it is Beethoven through and through.'

Unfortunately, the planned performance of the cantata failed to materialize. Perhaps the musicians simply found it too difficult – a recurring problem throughout Beethoven's career. Still, he knew the value of what he had done, and in later years he re-used some of the music in the final scene of his great liberation-opera *Fidelio*, where it does not seem to be in the least out of place.

Towards the end of 1790, Bonn received a distinguished musical guest, the composer Joseph Haydn, who was on his way from Vienna to London. Beethoven may well have met Haydn at a dinner given in his honour by the Elector. But it was when Haydn returned in 1792, after what turned out to be an enormously successful stay in London, that he realized what a musical force there was in the young court organist. Someone showed Haydn the score of the '*Joseph*' *Cantata* and he immediately agreed to accept Beethoven as a pupil. For Beethoven, this must indeed have come as excellent news. His hopes of studying with Mozart had been squashed when that brilliant and still young composer had died, tragically, in December 1791. He was only thirty-five. And now here was another great composer – one of the very few that Mozart himself had admired and even imitated – offering him lessons.

The Elector quickly granted Beethoven leave of absence and provided money towards his salary and expenses. Another important patron was Count Ferdinand von Waldstein, a man of cultivated musical tastes and something of a musician himself. He had arrived in Bonn in 1788 and had soon realized that Beethoven was exceptionally gifted. As Beethoven got ready for his trip to Vienna, Waldstein wrote these words in his private album:

Dear Beethoven,
You are now going to Vienna in fulfilment of a wish that has for
so long been thwarted. The genius of Mozart still mourns and
weeps for the death of its protégé. It has found a refuge in the
inexhaustible Haydn, but no permanent abode. Through him it
desires once more to find a union with someone. Through your
unceasing diligence, receive the spirit of Mozart from the hands
of Haydn.

Beethoven set off from Bonn on 2 November 1792. It was fortunate for him that he left when he did. Since the first stirrings of the French Revolution in 1789, the mood across Europe had grown increasingly uneasy. Then, in April 1792, the new French regime had declared war on Austria. By the time of Beethoven's departure, French forces had reached the Rhine and taken the city of Mainz.

In the early stages of his journey Beethoven saw plenty of evidence of the turmoil of war. In his account book there is a record of a special tip paid to the coachman, 'because the fellow drove us at the risk of a cudgelling right through the Hessian army, going like the devil.' Worse still, Beethoven and his travelling companion had only just avoided being cut off by French troops near the town of Limburg.

After that, however, things seem to have proceeded relatively smoothly. Beethoven arrived in Vienna on 10 November. His records show him equipping himself for his new life in the city: 'wood, wig, coffee, black silk stockings, overcoat, boots, shoes, piano-desk . . . '

He lost no time in establishing himself with the help of letters of introduction, particularly from Waldstein, and personal recommendations from Haydn. But if he intended to turn his back on his less pleasant memories of the Bonn years, events ruled otherwise.

In December 1792 came news of the death of his father, followed by the revelation that Johann had been pocketing the allowance intended for the composer's two younger brothers. Beethoven did not record his private feelings, although one can guess that they must have been fairly mixed.

But not all the memories of Bonn were sour or painful. In 1793, his first full year in Vienna, Beethoven wrote this characteristically self-assured, but also very generous tribute to the man who had been his greatest encouragement, his old teacher, Christian Neefe:

> *Thank you for the advice you have so often given me in the development of my God-given art. If I should ever become a great man, you too will have a share in my success.*

CHAPTER 2
A SECOND MOZART
(1792–1802)

+ *Beethoven's early friendships*
+ *First signs of deafness*

eethoven's biggest single emotional tie with Bonn was severed
with the death of Johann van Beethoven. There were still
Ludwig's two younger brothers, Caspar Carl (born 1774) and
Nikolaus Johann (born 1776), to be considered, but they were
showing encouraging signs of being able to look after themselves.
Both were soon to follow Ludwig to Vienna, Caspar Carl in 1794
and Nikolaus Johann in 1796. For a while, Caspar Carl also made
a moderately successful career as a musician, acting as assistant
to his elder brother and occasionally composing. But Nikolaus
Johann chose pharmacy, in which he prospered, particularly so
after he began his own business in the Upper Austrian city of Linz
in 1808.

Beethoven was still officially an employee of the Elector of
Bonn, but Maximilian Franz had other things on his mind. Bonn's
long period of prosperity and relative stability was coming to an
end. After the beheading of Louis XVI in 1792, revolutionary
France entered the 'Reign of Terror', with its mass executions of
political dissenters. Refugees flooded into Bonn, soon to be
followed by the French armies. As the brother of the hated Queen
Marie Antoinette, the figurehead of the counter-revolutionary
movement, Maximilian Franz knew he was high on the French
Government's hit-list. He fled Bonn in 1794, and with him went
Beethoven's official salary.

But things were going too well for Beethoven for him to be
greatly concerned by this loss of income. The death of Mozart in

1791 had left a hole at the heart of Viennese musical life, and Beethoven, already heralded in the musical press as 'a second Mozart', was singularly well-placed to fill it. His piano-playing was widely admired, and his compositions were catching the attention of some very influential connoisseurs. Prince Karl Lichnowsky, for instance, took such a proprietorial interest in Beethoven that, in 1793, he offered him rooms in his own house. Lichnowsky was to become the composer's leading patron during his early Viennese years. Every Friday evening he gave a concert at his home, at which Beethoven's music was frequently the centrepiece. Amongst the works heard there for the first time were Beethoven's official 'Opus 1', the three *Piano Trios* of 1794, which were duly dedicated to the Prince. Also dedicated to Lichnowsky were the *Piano Sonatas* Op.13 No.8 (the '*Pathétique*') and Op.26 No.12, and the *Second Symphony* Op.36 (1802).

Two other important new friendships were struck up at about this time. The word 'friendships' has to be stressed, for while Beethoven's relationships with his rich, aristocratic patrons may have been turbulent (Lichnowsky and Beethoven became virtually estranged for a while after 1806), they were frequently conducted on equal terms. Difficult as he was, Beethoven had an extraordinary ability to inspire admiration, loyalty, even love to those he dealt with. The Baron Nikolaus Zmeskall von Domanovecz, whom Beethoven first met around 1795, remained a close confidant even after he became bedridden in the 1820s.

Many of the letters Beethoven wrote to him have survived, and these often provide valuable insights. Zmeskall was also a great help to Beethoven in everyday matters, such as finding servants or paying off debts. A little before the first meeting with Zmeskall, Beethoven also got to know the Baron Gottfried van Swieten, friend and encourager of Mozart and a champion of the works of Bach (which Beethoven already knew) and Handel (which he didn't). Handel was to become increasingly important to Beethoven; in later years he was to say that Handel was 'the greatest composer that ever lived'. As a gesture of thanks to van Swieten for his practical and musical help, Beethoven dedicated his *First Symphony* Op.21 to him in 1800.

This is a good point to pause and examine one of the most interesting of the many contradictions in Beethoven's character. He was a believer in freedom, in the rights of man. Alongside an unconcealed desire for personal glory was a genuine hope that his work might in some way lead to a bettering of ordinary human conditions. In 1800 he told his old friend Franz Wegeler, with obvious feeling, that 'when the prosperity of our fatherland has improved, then my art must be directed towards the benefit of the poor. O happy moment, and how lucky I consider myself that I can contribute to this aim, that I myself can bring it to pass!' He left a vivid portrayal of tyranny in his opera *Fidelio*, and he was openly hostile to the increasingly repressive laws in Vienna and the reinstatement of some of the old aristocratic privileges. For the principle of heredity he had nothing but scorn: 'Prince,' he wrote to Lichnowsky, 'what you are, you are by accident of birth; what I am, I am of myself. There are and there will be thousands of princes. There is only one Beethoven.'

He made no attempt to hide his growing admiration for Napoleon. It is said that the Emperor Franz refused to have anything to do with Beethoven or his works; his reported verdict: 'There is something revolutionary in that music!'

Yet Lichnowsky, van Swieten, Zmeskall are only the beginning of a long line of aristocratic names closely associated with Beethoven. It is unlikely that he would have survived without their encouragement and their generous financial help. Beethoven's response was, on the whole, a characteristic mixture of intense, affectionate gratitude and sulky independence. One writer remembered how, on the grandest occasions, when everyone else was carefully powdered and peruked, Beethoven would often turn up 'dressed in the informal fashion of the other side of the Rhine, almost ill-dressed.' There were frequent quarrels or dramatic scenes, with Beethoven suddenly refusing to play to a room full of titled enthusiasts, or storming out, slamming the door; and just as frequently there were emotional reconciliations, impassioned apologies and promises of dedications, usually fulfilled.

And it is interesting to see how Beethoven dealt, or rather failed to deal, with a misunderstanding about his name. *Van* in Flemish/Dutch simply means 'from'; but in German *von* also signifies nobility, so for many Viennese, Ludwig *van* Beethoven was naturally understood to be a man of high social rank. Beethoven appears not to have made any great effort to correct this impression.

Emperor Franz had reason to be nervous of anything revolutionary. The influence of republican France was growing, and with it the threat of war. It was well known that Napoleon had his eye on Vienna. But at the same time the city was enjoying a cultural boom. Admittedly a lot of the activity was of a frivolous kind (perhaps 'escapist' would be a better description). This was the age that saw the rise of the waltz (the 'lascivious waltz', as it was repeatedly called) in the place of the old, stately minuet. Beethoven was by no means unresponsive to this new market. In November 1795 he provided twelve minuets and twelve examples of the 'German Dance' (an ancestor of the waltz) for the masked ball of the Society of Artists at the Redoutensaal. But there was a large, responsive audience for his serious work, too. Later that same year he gave a performance of the first version of his monumental *First Piano Concerto* Op.15. It was a great success, despite Beethoven's complaints of sickness, and despite his completing the Finale only two days before the concert.

As an improviser, Beethoven was a sensation. Improvising competitions were arranged. One challenger, the Abbé Gelinek, confessed afterwards: 'Satan himself is hidden in that young man. I have never heard anyone play like that!' In 1800 there came a more impressive challenge, from the then much admired pianist-composer Daniel Steibelt. As an act of deliberate provocation, Steibelt chose a theme of Beethoven's to improvise on and then, confident of victory, waited for Beethoven's response. Beethoven picked up the cello part of Steibelt's own *Quintet*, stuck it, roughly, upside down on the piano, and proceeded to improvise so brilliantly and mockingly that Steibelt walked out in mid-performance and refused to meet him ever again.

But it wasn't simply for brilliance, audacity or wild imagination that Beethoven the pianist was admired. His pupil Carl Czerny remembered his 'new type of singing tone', and how his slow movements in particular were 'spirited, grandiose . . . very full of feeling and romantic. His performance, like his compositions, was a tone-painting of a very high order and conceived only for a total effect.'

Some, however, had their doubts, and not only those who, like Steibelt, Beethoven had offended. The Bohemian composer Václav Tomásek admired the playing, but had his doubts about the composing. After Beethoven's visit to Prague in 1796, he wrote that: 'His frequent daring deviations from one motif to another, by which the organic cohesion, the gradual development of idea was broken up, did not escape me. Evils of this kind often weaken his best compositions.' But even the doubters had to admit that here was a real musical force, and one with a very bright future. One reviewer wrote:

> *He seems already to have penetrated to the inner sanctuary of music. . . . A living proof of his genuine love of art emerges from the fact that he has put himself in the charge of our immortal Haydn so as to be initiated in the holy secrets of the art of music. The latter great master, during his absence, has handed him over to the great Albrechtsburger. What cannot be expected when such a genius commits himself into the hands of such excellent masters!*

That reference to Haydn 'handing [Beethoven] over to the great Albrechtsberger' neatly conceals a fraught situation. Officially, Beethoven was Haydn's pupil. But Haydn was easy-going, gently paternal, by no means a stickler or a disciplinarian. Beethoven, on the other hand, was intense, demanding and aloof at the same time, his pride easily wounded. He was a free spirit, and yet he wanted discipline, strictness. He misinterpreted Haydn's relaxed manner as slackness and neglect and, typically, forgot Haydn's many kind acts, such as his introduction to his patron, the very musical and immensely wealthy Prince Nikolaus Esterházy. Some time before Haydn left for his second trip to London in 1794, Beethoven had secretly begun to take lessons with the theorist Johann Schenk. When Beethoven took up with Albrechtsberger he worked hard at the most rigorous exercises his teacher could set him. As if this wasn't enough, he also sought tuition from the composer Emanuel Aloys Förster and later approached Antonio Salieri – still famous as an opera composer – for advice in writing for the voice.

After Haydn's return, relations between the two composers curdled, especially after Haydn made what appeared to be a mildly critical remark about Beethoven's *C minor Piano Trio* Op.1 No.3. Haydn praised the Op.1 set as a whole, but advised Beethoven not to publish the C minor. According to Beethoven's friend Ferdinand Ries, Haydn was simply being practical: this was an important publication for the young composer, and he doubted that the C minor work 'would have been so quickly and easily understood and so favourably received by the public' as the other two would be.

Typically, Beethoven over-reacted. First, he claimed that Haydn had tried to prevent the publication because he was jealous. Later he was to claim that he had learnt nothing at all from Haydn – a transparently ridiculous remark, since the older man's music certainly left its mark on the young composer. Haydn, too, was a brilliantly imaginative composer and one who loved surprise (this was the creator of the '*Surprise*' *Symphony*), but at the same time he had a profound understanding of musical logic. However startling his ideas may seem, they are rarely mere 'effects'; there is a reason for them, a hidden sense, as the perceptive listener soon discovers. Without Haydn's example it is possible that Beethoven would have taken much longer to reach that remarkable balance of originality and profound formal strength for which he is so much admired today, and which Czerny must have sensed when he spoke of Beethoven's feeling for the 'total effect'. And surely it cannot be without significance that the musical forms in which Haydn excelled – the symphony, the piano sonata and the string quartet – were also central to Beethoven's output. The kinship ran deeper than Beethoven was prepared to admit, at least at that time.

Whatever his difficulties in finding satisfactory teaching, for Beethoven the composer the first decade in Vienna was to be a period of tremendous growth and enrichment. In the first move-ment of the '*Pathétique*' *Sonata* (1798), Beethoven's tragic-heroic C minor mode stands before us, fully rounded, for the first time. The dark, slow introduction, marked 'Grave', is one of the most arresting beginnings in all piano music, and the alternations between this and the hurtling, anguished 'Allegro' represent a new kind of musical drama. But not long after this comes some-thing utterly different: the *Septet* Op.20 (begun 1799) for clarinet, bassoon, horn, violin, viola, cello and double bass. A lovely, effort-lessly humorous piece, it was to become one of the most popular of all Beethoven's works in his own lifetime – so much so that Beethoven, ever contrary, grew to resent it.

At this time, Beethoven began his first set of string quartets; it was the custom at that time to offer quartets in groups of three or six. The influence of the great quartets of Haydn and Mozart is evident, but more striking are the forward-looking elements, particularly the Finale of Op.18 No.6, which veers between a cheerful 'Allegretto' and disturbed, slow music, headed by 'La Malinconia' (Melancholy). The 'Allegretto' music prevails at the end, but memories of 'La Malinconia' linger uncomfortably. Beethoven was to explore this kind of ambiguity repeatedly in later works.

There is another fascinating revelation in the first of the Op.18 *Quartets*. Two versions survive and as anyone who compares them closely will see, the second is in almost every respect an improvement. Beethoven could compose quickly, and he had no difficulty producing arresting effects. But that wasn't enough: he wanted clarity and that profound formal logic he had sensed in Bach, Mozart and Haydn. That required hard work. In his sketch-books he can be observed trying ideas over and over again, changing them sometimes minutely, sometimes radically, and carefully balancing part against whole. Hearing the two versions of Op.18 No.1 we can see how Beethoven had begun to become his own teacher – and a very critical and demanding one.

It is a clear sign of Beethoven's growing confidence as a composer that at the same time as he was working on his Op.18 *Quartets*, he also completed his *First Symphony* Op.21 (1800). An earlier attempt at a symphony (1795) had been abandoned early on. The First Symphony was premiered, with the *Septet*, in a concert at the Burgtheater on 2 April 1800. The *First Piano Concerto* Op.15 was also played, and Beethoven improvised. The concerto was a great success, the septet and the improvisation still more so, but reactions to the symphony were more mixed. One problem was that the orchestra, made up of musicians from the Italian Opera, was simply not good enough.

This may seem difficult to believe now, when youth orchestras quite happily take on Beethoven's most challenging orchestral works, but for orchestral players at the end of the eighteenth century, this was unusually difficult music not only to play, but to understand. The very first chord of the symphony is a surprise: it is in the 'wrong' key. Beethoven quickly and elegantly corrects this deliberate mistake, but the device seems to have been too clever for some of the players, and for many of the audience. It was one thing to play tricks like this in a connoisseur's medium like the string quartet, but in the more public arena of an orchestral concert, it was new.

Still, whatever doubts there may have been about this or that individual work, Beethoven would seem to have had every reason to count himself a success. He was in demand as player and as composer both with specialist audiences and with the general musical public, and he was making money from his music. Some of the things he did were controversial, but in a way that most people seem to have found stimulating. In our time, he would be the kind of figure who is rarely out of the Sunday supplements. The fact that he had not yet been able to marry was a source of frustration: his first known proposal, to a singer named Magdalena Willmann, had been rejected because the lady in question found her suitor 'ugly and half-crazy'; but while Beethoven was no Adonis, quite a number of women seem to have found him fascinating and sexually attractive. Surely it was only a matter of time.

Privately, however, there was a disturbing development. In a letter of May 1797 to Franz Wegeler, now a practising doctor, Beethoven expresses intense relief over his 'improving health'. What the trouble was he doesn't say, but some think this might have been the beginning of a much bigger problem, one that was to make Beethoven's life almost unbearable and perhaps, at times, even to threaten his sanity.

One of the first hints comes in a recollection by Carl Czerny. The ten-year-old Czerny was taken to Beethoven's apartments in the winter of 1799–1800 to see if the composer would be interested in giving him piano lessons. He remembered 'a very barren-looking room, with papers and clothes thrown about all over the place, a few bare walls, hardly a single chair except for a wobbly one by the piano, a Walter, at that time the best available.' And then there was the great man himself:

> ... dressed in a jacket of some shaggy dark-grey cloth, with trousers of the same material. ... The pitch-black hair stood up on his head. His beard, unshaven for several days, blackened the lower part of his already dark-complexioned face. I also noticed at a glance, as children often do, that his ears were stuffed with cotton-wool which seemed to have been dipped in some kind of yellow liquid.

Another letter to Wegeler, written slightly later, reveals the truth at last. 'During the last three years my hearing has become weaker and weaker. The problem seems to be caused by the state of my abdomen, which, as you know, was dreadful even before I left Bonn, but which has become still worse in Vienna.' This was an appalling discovery for a musician; but for Beethoven the consequence in simple human terms was just as bad. A composer can write in his or her head. Some can manage without any recourse to musical instruments – one or two have even preferred to work that way – and Beethoven often found his ideas while out walking, away from the keyboard. And for the moment it did not interfere with his performing. 'When I am playing and compos- ing', he told another friend, the violinist Karl Friedrich Amenda, 'my affliction troubles me least; it affects me most when I am in company.' Difficult as he may have been socially, Beethoven loved conversation, especially with lively or witty people; if they were female, better still. The thought of losing this terrified him, and he begged Wegeler and Amenda to keep knowledge of his condi- tion to themselves.

A cure had to be found. The letters to Wegeler are full of urgent questions. Bathing in tepid Danube water had been suggested – would that help? What about this 'galvanism' (elec- tromagnetism) that was supposed to have had miraculous effects in Berlin? And what about the suggestion, made by a prominent Viennese doctor, that pieces of bark, strapped to the arms, might provide a cure?

Perhaps the best remedy was simply rest. It was the custom in Vienna (for those with money) to spend the summer months in one of the small villages which at that time lay just outside the city. Beethoven would do the same. He had just begun another symphony, his second, and it promised to be a still more original and ambitious work than its predecessor. What could be better than to take it with him to a quiet lodging in pleasant surround- ings, and there let nature take its course?

So, in April 1802, Beethoven set out for the village of Heili- genstadt, to the north of Vienna. Thanks to an extraordinary document that he wrote during his stay there, we know what the consequences were.

CHAPTER 3

THE HERO
(1802–12)

- ◆ The Heiligenstadt Testament
- ◆ The 'Eroica' Symphony
- ◆ Meeting with Goethe
- ◆ Immortal Beloveds

A revealing document, written by the composer to his brothers from the village of Heiligenstadt in 1802, was discovered only after Beethoven's death, twenty-five years later. Known today as the Heiligenstadt Testament, it demonstrates much of the composer's hidden torment.

For my brothers Carl and [Johann] B

O ye men, who consider or declare me to be hostile, obstinate or misanthropic, how unjust you are to me, for you do not know the secret cause of that which makes me seem so to you. My heart and my soul, since my childhood, have ever been filled with tender feelings of good will: I was even ready to perform great deeds. But consider that for six years now I have been afflicted with an incurable condition, made worse by incompetent physicians, deceived for year after year by the hope of an improvement and now obliged to face the prospect of a permanent disability (the healing of which may take years or may even prove to be quite impossible). Born with an ardent, lively temperament and also inclined to the distractions of society, I was, at an early age, obliged to seclude myself and live my life in solitude. If, once in a while, I attempted to ignore all this, oh how harshly would I be driven back by the doubly sad experience of my bad hearing; yet it was not possible for me to say: speak louder, shout, because I am deaf. Alas, how would it be possible for me to admit to a weakness of the one sense that should be perfect to a higher degree in me than in others, the one sense which I once possessed in the highest perfection, a perfection that few others of my profession have ever possessed. No, I cannot do it. So forgive me if you see me draw back from your company which I would so gladly share. My misfortune is doubly hard to bear, inasmuch as I will surely be misunderstood. For me there can be no recreation in the society of others, no intelligent conversation, no mutual exchange of ideas; only as much as is required by the most pressing needs can I venture into society. I am obliged to live like an outcast. If I venture into the company of men, I am overcome with a burning terror, inasmuch as I fear to find myself in the danger of allowing my condition to be noticed. So it has been for this last half year which I have spent in the country. Advised by my sensible physician to spare my hearing as much as possible, he to a certain extent encouraged my natural disposition: although sometimes torn by the desire for companionship, I allowed myself to be tempted into it. But what a humiliation when someone standing next to me could hear in the distance the sound of a flute whereas I heard nothing. Or someone could hear the shepherd singing, and that I also did not hear. Such experiences brought me near to despair, it would have needed little for me to put an end to my life. It was art only which held me back. Ah, it seemed to me impossible to leave the world before I had brought forth all that I felt destined to bring forth. So I endured this miserable existence – miserable indeed. For I have so sensitive a body that even a slight change can transport me from the highest to the most wretched states. Patience – it is said – is what I must now choose as my guide. This I have done – and I hope that my resolution will remain firm until the implacable Parcae are pleased to break the thread. Perhaps my condition will improve – perhaps it will not. I am obliged – when only in my twenty-eighth year [sic] – to become a philosopher, and that is not easy, and for an artist it is harder than for any other. Almighty God, Thou lookest down into my innermost being; Thou knowest that the love of mankind and the desire to do good dwell therein. Oh, men, when you once shall read *this, reflect then, that you have wronged me, and let some unfortunate be comforted that he has found one like himself who, in the face of all the obstacles which nature has placed in his path, has yet done all that lay in his power to be numbered among the ranks of worthy artists and men – You, my brothers, Carl and [Johann], as soon as I am dead, if Doctor Schmidt be still alive, request him in my name to describe my malady, and let him attach this written document to the report of my ailment, so that, as far as possible, the world may be reconciled with me after my death. At the same time I hereby declare both of you to be the heirs of my small estate (if such it can be termed), divide it justly, bear with and help each other. What harm you have done to me, that, you know, has long since been forgiven. I thank you, my brother Carl in particular, for the affection which you have shown me in these latter times. My wish is that you may lead a better life and one more free of care than mine. Recommend* virtue *to your children: that alone, and not money, can ensure happiness. I speak from experience: it was virtue which sustained me in my misery; next I thank my art that I did not end my life in suicide. Farewell – love each other. I thank all my friends, in particular* Prince Lichnowsky *and* Doctor Schmidt. *I wish the instruments from Prince L. to be preserved by one of you, but no quarrel between you should arise over them. In the event that they may serve a more useful purpose, sell them by all means. How happy I am if even in my grave I may be of help to you. So it has come to pass. I go to meet my death joyfully. If it comes before I have had the opportunity to fulfil all my artistic destiny, then, despite my hard fate, it shall have come too soon, and I shall wish that it had come later. Nevertheless, I shall be content, for will it not free me from a condition of endless suffering? Come* when *thou willst. I go bravely to meet thee. Farewell, and do not forget me wholly. I deserve it from you, since in life I have often given thought of how to make you happy. Be ye so.*

Ludwig van Beethoven

Heiglnstadt [sic] on 6th October, 1802

Heiglnstadt on 10th October 1802 thus I take leave of you – and sadly too – Yes, the fond hope which I brought here with me that at least I might be healed to a certain extent – I now abandon forever, like the leaves in Autumn, fallen and withering on the ground – so is that hope blighted – I leave this place almost as I came – even that high courage – which often inspired me in the beautiful days of summer – it has now vanished. Oh Providence, vouchsafe me at least one single day of pure joy! For so long now has that inner echo of true joy been denied to me – When, oh when oh Divine Godhead – shall I once feel it in the Temple of Nature and among mankind. Never? – No, that would be too hard.

For my brothers Carl and [Johann] to be read and executed after my death.

♦

Of all the intriguing questions that surround the 'Heiligenstadt Testament' (why, for instance, are there blank spaces where Johann's name should be?), perhaps the most pressing is simply: what exactly did Beethoven mean it to be? Is it a will, a suicide note, a 'cry for help', or a purely private meditation? Different parts suggest different interpretations. It is, however, almost certain that Beethoven's brothers never saw this document.

Plenty has been written about the 'Heiligenstadt Testament', not all of it admiring. Some commentators have found it melodramatic; others have suggested that Beethoven may have revised it, that the published version was his 'fair copy', tidied up for the benefit of posterity. But parts of it are still very moving, and the repeated mention of death more than hints at a desperate state of mind.

While encroaching deafness was the central problem, there may have been other contributory factors. The dedication of the so-called '*Moonlight*' *Sonata* Op.27 No.2 provides a clue.

This deeply personal piece, with its quietly impassioned first movement and tempestuous Finale, was offered to a pupil, the Countess Giulietta Guicciardi, in 1801. A letter to Franz Wegeler from that time mentions that he has found some comfort in a 'dear charming girl who loves me and whom I love' – almost certainly Giulietta. But the relationship – whatever form it took – did not last, and by 1803 Giulietta had married someone more socially acceptable, the Count von Gallenberg. Some remarks written towards the end of his life suggest that Beethoven was deeply hurt by Giulietta's desertion. Could that have been another influence on the dark mood of the 'Heiligenstadt Testament'?

It is tempting to see something of this same black depression in two works Beethoven wrote at about this time: the *Violin Sonata in C minor* Op.30 No.2, and the *D minor Piano Sonata* Op.31 No.2. But this is too simple. For every one work in which the composer's anguished feelings seem to pour out onto the page, there are others that are, emotionally speaking, worlds apart.

Take the *Second Symphony* Op.36, which Beethoven probably worked on at Heiligenstadt in that summer of 1802. The symphony has its darker moments – in the culminating coda of the first movement there is a sense of real struggle – but the overwhelming impression is of a bright, positive, joyful work, especially in the Finale. The mood of the 'Heiligenstadt Testament' seems impossibly remote.

The fact is that composing need not only be self-expression; it can also be self-transformation, or even self-transcendence. There is a telling sentence in the 'Heiligenstadt Testament': 'It was *art* only that held me back.' In another letter to Wegeler Beethoven exclaims: 'I will take fate by the throat. It will certainly not bend or crush me completely.' Perhaps that is what we can hear in the *Second Symphony*'s first movement; and in some of the works that followed it that determination is more strongly evident. It is through his art that Beethoven will 'take fate by the throat'. The opening lines of a poem by W.B. Yeats could have been written specifically for him:

> *The intellect of man is forced to choose*
> *Perfection of the life, or of the work,*
> *And if it take the second must refuse*
> *A heavenly mansion, raging in the dark.*

Whatever Beethoven may have thought or felt at the time of the Testament, his mood seems to have changed radically when he returned to Vienna. Just over a week after the date of the Heiligenstadt postscript he was writing excitedly to a publisher about his two new sets of *Piano Variations*, Opp.34 & 35, which, he claims are 'written in a completely new manner'.

And a month later his old pugnaciousness was back with a vengeance. When he discovered that his *String Quintet* Op.29 had been sold, by some mistake, to two different publishers, he sabotaged the proofs of one edition and then published a savage attack on that same publisher for allowing the mistakes to happen. There was a court case and Beethoven lost, but he never published a full retraction.

The creative expansion continued. So far Beethoven had written no large-scale vocal works since the '*Joseph II*' *Cantata* of 1790 and its companion piece, '*Cantata on the accession of Emperor Leopold II*', of the same year. But now, provoked perhaps by the recent success of Haydn's oratorio *The Seasons*, and encouraged by his recent appointment as composer in residence at the Theatre an der Wien, Beethoven set to work on a grand oratorio of his own: '*Christ on the Mount of Olives*', Op.85. Like many of Beethoven's works of this time it was written very quickly (February–March 1803) and at the same as he was working on another major score: the revised version of the *Third Piano Concerto* Op.37. *Christ on the Mount of Olives* was premiered in April 1803.

Neither the audience nor the critics were enthusiastic. The text was universally condemned; some felt that Beethoven's music redeemed at least parts of it, but the writer August von Kotzebue evidently spoke for many when he complained that the vocal writing lacked 'expressive relevance'. Even Beethoven appears to have agreed: his own reported verdict was that it had been 'a mistake to have treated the role of Christ in a modern operatic manner.'

As for the verdict of posterity, *Christ on the Mount of Olives* is generally judged more interesting as a precursor to Beethoven's one great opera, *Fidelio*, than as a work in its own right – a 'rehearsal', one writer has called it. But there is nothing in the least rehearsal-like about the works that followed. In April 1803 the young virtuoso violinist George Polgreen Bridgetower arrived in Vienna. Bridgetower was a sensational violinist and of added interest to an early nineteenth-century European audience, he was a mulatto, the son of an African father and a Polish mother. Beethoven was deeply impressed by Bridgetower and immediately began writing a violin and piano sonata for him. On the title page he wrote: 'Mulattic Sonata. Composed for the mulatto Brischdauer, great lunatic and mulattic composer.'

The result was the *Sonata in A* Op.47, a brilliant and sometimes explosively emotional work, which is still one of Beethoven's most popular chamber pieces. Beethoven and Bridgetower gave the first performance together in May. As with the *First Piano Concerto*, the music was only just ready on time and Bridgetower had to play from Beethoven's manuscript – a heroic task in itself. If anyone could be said to have earned his dedication, it was Bridgetower, but it was not to be. Soon afterwards the two men fell out (apparently over a woman) and the work went to another violinist, Rodolphe Kreutzer. Ever since, it has been known as the '*Kreutzer*' *Sonata*.

Then, between June and October 1803, Beethoven produced one of his greatest works, his *Third Symphony* Op.55, the '*Eroica*' ('Heroic'). It has cast a huge shadow: right up to the present day, composers have admitted to feeling intimidated by its power and total mastery. Once again, there is story behind the dedication. The final inscription was to Prince Franz Joseph von Lobkowitz, but originally Beethoven had intended the score for none other than Napoleon Bonaparte, which was quite a courageous thing to do in Emperor Franz's increasingly repressive Vienna. But then, in May 1804, Beethoven heard news that astonished and enraged him. Napoleon had proclaimed himself Emperor of France. In a fury he took the title page of the 'Eroica' and obliterated Napoleon's name. 'So he too is nothing more than an ordinary man', he told his friend and pupil Ferdinand Ries. 'Now he will trample on all human rights and indulge only his own ambition. He will place himself above everyone and become a tyrant.'

Cruel as it must have been for Beethoven, it is fortunate for us that his disillusionment came so soon. If the *Third Symphony* had remained the 'Napoleon Bonaparte' Symphony no doubt all kinds of crude pictorial programmes might have been suggested for it – the kind of thing that Beethoven himself came to hate. Instead, we can hear the symphony as a work about heroism itself, not of the military kind, but something deeper, the will to overcome or simply endure difficulties – fear, pain, inner turmoil, the terror of death. Examining the sketchbooks, one can see that even the process of composing had a heroic quality. The theme of the 'Funeral March' second movement, for instance, went through many transformations before it arrived at the sharply etched, deeply expressive form we know now. Sometimes Beethoven's first ideas are not very promising, but he persisted, as though he realized that somewhere, hidden in this or that scrap of a motif, was the embryo of a great idea.

For many, the '*Eroica*' is the greatest of all purely orchestral symphonies. Like many of the symphonies of Mahler, it seems to contain a universe of contrasts: there is the momentous drama of the first movement with its exultant coda; the Funeral March, grand at first, then seemingly broken by grief; then comes the airborne dance of the Scherzo, followed by the epic variation-Finale, drawing together humour, upheaval, intimate poetry, a retrospective glance at the dark heart of the March, and then an eruption of defiant joy – as though the symphony were determined to rejoice. The miracle is that somehow all of this is drawn together in a living, formal framework of cast-iron strength.

The '*Eroica*' was too new, too ambitious, even simply too big for some members of its first audience. One reviewer, although sympathetic, complained that there was 'too much that is shrill and bizarre, whereby an overall view is made difficult and any sense of unity is almost completely absent' – not a view that would find broad agreement today. But Beethoven seems to have been unaffected by this adverse criticism. A stream of marvellous works followed the 'Eroica' and, to his delight, Beethoven began to find that he could make a living simply by composing (he had almost given up performing by this stage); he could afford servants, wine, good lodgings, just about everything he needed for a comfortable life. Two magnificent piano sonatas date from 1804–5: the '*Waldstein*' Op.53 No.21, dedicated to Beethoven's first important patron, and the aptly named '*Appassionata*', Op.57 No.23. But at the same time another, still grander project was keeping Beethoven busy – an opera.

Like *Christ on the Mount of Olives*, *Leonore* – as it was originally entitled – grew out of Beethoven's partnership with Emanuel Schikaneder, manager of the Theater an der Wien and famous as the author of the text of Mozart's *The Magic Flute*. The story of a political prisoner, rescued by his wife from death at the hands of a tryannical and dangerously ambitious prison governor, had a strong attraction for Beethoven. Perhaps, in addition to the political message, there was a personal appeal: a man, imprisoned alone, in darkness, is saved and brought back to life and the light of day by a loyal, beautiful woman. Beethoven's passionate involvement in the final hymn to the faithful Leonore and her like is unmistakeable.

This time the political content got Beethoven into trouble: the official censor refused to certify *Leonore* for performance. An appeal by the librettist, Joseph Sonnleithner, was eventually successful. 'It is true that a Minister abuses his powers', Sonnleithner argued, 'but only to indulge in private revenge – in Spain – in the sixteenth century.' But this was a minor inconvenience compared with what happened next. The efforts of the Viennese to ignore the growing international turmoil were finally quashed when the French armies, headed by Napoleon himself, arrived in Vienna. Napoleon commandeered the Imperial Palace of Schönbrunn and set about imposing his rule on the city. *Leonore* was performed, but to an audience composed almost entirely of the French military, who appear to have found it a colossal bore. The opera closed after three nights.

Almost immediately Beethoven set about revising both music and text, the latter with the help of his old friend Stephan von Breuning. The new version was tried again, after things had quietened down a little, in March 1806, and again it failed. At first Beethoven was quick to place the blame on the performers: 'All desire to compose anything further ceases completely if I have to hear my work performed like that!' For the second time he withdrew the score.

But the flood of masterpieces continued. In 1806 Beethoven began work on the three so-called '*Razumovsky*' *String Quartets* Op.59, to be dedicated to Count Andrei Kirillovich Razumovsky, Ambassador to the Austrian court. One commentator wrote that Razumovsky was 'less famous, perhaps, for his diplomacy than notorious for the profuseness of his expenditures, and for his amours with women of the highest rank, the queen of Naples not excepted.' But he was also a man of cultivated musical taste who, in 1808, was to set up his own string quartet with some of the finest players available at the time.

Inspired by the thought of writing for such an intelligent connoisseur and for such able musicians, Beethoven became still more adventurous: the first and third of the Op.59 *Quartets* are particularly innovative, while Op.59 No.2 contains one of his most spellbindingly beautiful slow movements, said to be inspired by the words of the great German philosopher Immanuel Kant: 'The starry heavens above, the moral law within.' As a special tribute to Count Razumovsky, Beethoven included Russian folk tunes in Op.59 Nos.1 & 2, although what he does with them is utterly personal.

Still more than the '*Eroica*' *Symphony*, the '*Razumovsky*' *Quartets* astonished and baffled their first audiences. Carl Czerny remembered how the scherzo second movement of Op.59 No.1, with its strange, repeated-note opening motif, set the audience off laughing: they 'were convinced that Beethoven was playing a joke'. Another prominent musician pronounced that 'these Quartets are not music'. Today, musicians and critics see them very differently. Op.59 No.1 has been compared to the '*Eroica*' *Symphony* in stature for, like the '*Eroica*', it is bigger and more formally ambitious than any work written before in that medium. A sketch for Op.59 No.3 hints at a possible autobiographical significance: over the fugal theme of the Finale, which springs suddenly and with tremendous energy, from the dying moments of the Minuet third movement, Beethoven wrote, 'Let your deafness no longer be a secret.'

Beethoven's productivity in that year, 1806, is astonishing. As well as the three '*Razumovsky*' *Quartets* and the second version of *Leonore*, he wrote the *Fourth Symphony* Op.60 and the *Violin Concerto* Op.61 and completed the *Fourth Piano Concerto* Op.58. Far from resting, in 1807 he went on to produce the *Mass in C* Op.86, the Overture *Coriolan* Op.62, and the work which, above all others, seems to epitomize his attempt to 'take fate by the throat', the *Fifth Symphony* Op.67.

From its very opening bars – probably the most famous beginning to a symphony in history – the first movement of the Fifth is an intense, ferociously driven exploration of Beethoven's tragic-heroic C minor mode. In the Scherzo third movement this mood is recalled, but then comes a remarkable passage: over quiet, repeated drum taps the Scherzo theme fragments and then builds a huge crescendo, at the height of which the full orchestra, amplified by trombones (their first ever use in a symphony), hammers out a new theme in a triumphant C major – the Finale has begun. Later the Scherzo theme returns, in an eerie pizzicato version, only to be swept out of the way again by the Finale theme. Beethoven has linked movements before (in Op.59 Nos.1 & 3, for instance), but this kind of fusion, in which the drama of one movement is inextricably bound up with that of its predecessor, was quite new.

Another symphony followed in 1808, the '*Pastoral*' Op.68, as unlike the Fifth as could be imagined, despite the return of the trombones. The five movements (another new formal departure) are a magnificent summation of Beethoven's love of nature and the open country. It is full of evocations of sounds for which the increasingly deaf composer must have had to rely on his long-term memory: bird-song in the 'Scene by a brook', rural dances in 'Peasants merry-making' and a shepherd's pipe in the Finale – remember the remark about the unheard shepherd in the Heiligenstadt Testament. There is also a thrilling 'Storm' movement. But what makes the 'Pastoral' different from the many other 'pastoral' pieces that appeared at about that time is the depth of the feeling expressed – Beethoven always insisted that *this*, not tone-painting, was what the symphony was really about.

By the middle of 1808 there was such a backlog of new, unplayed work that Beethoven realized he would have to arrange performances himself. The result was a mammoth concert, at the Theater an der Wien, on 22 December. The programme included the *Fifth* and *Sixth Symphonies*, the *Fourth Piano Concerto*, movements from the *Mass in C*, the concert aria '*Ah! Perfido!*' Op.65, a piano improvisation by Beethoven, and a work specially composed for the concert, the *Choral Fantasia* for piano, chorus and orchestra Op.80.

It was the stuff of which nightmares are made. A guest of Prince Lobkowitz, the travel writer Johann Friedrich Reichardt, left a vivid account of the evening:

> *There we sat, in the most bitter cold, from half past six until half past ten, and confirmed the old adage that you can easily have too much of a good thing, still more of a powerful one.*
>
> *... Poor Beethoven, who had his first and only ready profit of the whole year from this concert, met considerable hostility and only feeble support in the arrangements and the performance. Singers and orchestra were made up of very mixed elements, and it wasn't even possible to arrange one full rehearsal of all the pieces in the programme, every one of which was filled with the greatest difficulties. Nevertheless, the quantity of work by this fruitful genius and tireless worker which was performed in those four hours will astonish you.*
>
> *To begin, a pastoral symphony, or recollections of country life.... Each number was a very long and fully worked-out movement, filled with liveliest images and the most brilliant ideas and motifs; in consequence, this one pastoral symphony lasted longer than a whole concert is permitted to last with us.*

After this came:

> *a long Italian scena* [Ah! Perfido!], *sung by Mlle Killizky, the lovely Bohemian with the lovely voice. That this pretty girl rather shivered than sang was hardly surprising, given the bitter cold; in our box near by, we too were shivering, wrapped in our furs and greatcoats.*

Next,

> *a Gloria, with choruses and solos; the performance, alas, failed completely.*

There followed:

> *a new concerto for piano, terrifyingly difficult, which Beethoven played brilliantly and as fast as possible. In the Adagio, a masterpiece of beautiful sustained melody, he actually seemed to make his instrument sing with deep melancholy feeling which awakened strong feelings within me.*

Next,

> *a great symphony, very elaborate and too long.*

After that,

> *a Sanctus, again with choruses and solo numbers, again – like the Gloria – a complete failure in performance.*

Following the Sanctus,

> *a long fantasy, in which Beethoven revealed the full extent of his mastery.*
>
> *And finally . . . another fantasy, in which the orchestra joined in and was eventually followed by the chorus. This strange idea met with disaster in performance as the result of an orchestral chaos so complete that Beethoven, with all the fervour of the true artist, forgetting his public or even where he was, shouted that they must stop and begin again. You can imagine how much I and all his other friends suffered at this. At that moment, I began to wish that I'd had the courage to leave earlier on.*

Did the monumental failure of the Theatre an der Wien concert make Beethoven consider leaving Vienna? If so, that might explain why, when the offer of a post as *Kapellmeister* came from the German city of Kassel in January 1809, he very nearly accepted, even though this would have meant working for Napoleon's brother Jerome, who had been created 'King of Westphalia' in the new French empire. Realizing that they might lose him, a group of Beethoven's aristocratic friends got together to offer him money to keep him in Vienna. Generous and well-timed though this offer was, Beethoven drove a hard bargain. In the end, a contract was signed guaranteeing him an annual salary of 4,000 florins: 1,800 from Prince Kinsky, 1,500 from the Archduke Rudolph and 700 from Prince Lobkowitz. The contract also stipulated annual use of the Theater an der Wien.

In terms of Beethoven's career, Prince Kinsky was a relative newcomer, and his involvement with the composer was to end when he was killed in a horse-riding accident in 1812. Beethoven dedicated the *Mass in C* to him after Prince Nikolaus Esterházy, for whom it was originally intended, found it 'unbearably ridiculous and detestable'.

Archduke Rudolph was to be involved with Beethoven for much longer. He was the youngest son of Leopold II and the brother of the reactionary Emperor Franz, but he didn't share Franz's apprehensions about Beethoven or his music. A fine pianist and a talented composer, he was a pupil of Beethoven from about 1803, and he became a lifelong friend and patron.

Beethoven dedicated more works to Archduke Rudolph than to anyone else; the list includes such outstanding compositions as the *Fourth* and *Fifth Piano Concertos* Opp.58 & 73, the '*Hammerklavier*' (Op.106 No.29) and Op.111 No.32 *Piano Sonatas*, the *Violin Sonata* Op.96, the so-called '*Archduke*' *Piano Trio* Op.97, the *Missa Solemnis* Op.123, the *Große Fuge* for string quartet Op.133, and the *Piano Sonata* '*Les Adieux*' ('The Farewells'), Op.81a No.26, whose three movements express the full range of Beethoven's feelings at the departure, absence and return of Rudolph between 1809 and 1810.

Why did the Archduke leave Vienna then? For a very sound, practical reason. After their occupation of Vienna 1805–6, the French had left peacefully enough. But now they were returning in force. Austria had declared war on France in April 1809, but had been unable to keep Napoleon at bay. The French began to surround Vienna in May and almost immediately the bombardment began. Beethoven hid in his brother Carl's cellar, clutching pillows to his ears in an effort to save what remained of his hearing. The occupation lasted only two months, but this time it left its mark. 'What a destructive, disordered life I see and hear around me', wrote Beethoven: 'nothing but drums, cannons and human misery in every form.'

Also during the occupation, Haydn had died, at the age of seventy-seven. By then Beethoven had forgotten their earlier tensions. After a performance of Haydn's *The Creation* in 1808 he had, it was reported, knelt and kissed his old teacher's hand. Later he would happily speak of him in the same breath as his revered Mozart and Handel.

After the occupation Beethoven's remarkable musical fertility continued. Now there was more chamber music, but there were grander projects too, such as the Overture and incidental music, Op.84, to *Egmont*, by the poet and playwright Johann Wolfgang von Goethe.

The story – the heroic resistance of a Flemish nobleman to Spanish oppression – must have stirred Beethoven deeply. He was much attracted to Goethe. He had set to music three of Goethe's poems in 1809, and later he was to speak with great enthusiasm of the possibility of providing music for *Faust*, one of the great musical might-have-beens.

Beethoven finally met Goethe at Teplitz, near the spa town of Karlsbad, in the summer of 1812. Goethe's written judgements of Beethoven vary. To his friend Karl Zelter he wrote:

> *His talent astounded me; but unfortunately he is a quite intractable person, which in fact is not unjustified if he finds the world detestable; but as a result, of course, he does not make things more enjoyable either for himself or for others. He is much to be forgiven and also to be pitied, since he can hear nothing.*

But to his wife, that same year, Goethe wrote that he had 'never before met a more comprehensive, energetic or intense artist. There is an eye-witness account of the first meeting between Goethe and Beethoven, and if the picture it paints is reliable, it is easy to see why Goethe felt uncomfortable in the composer's presence. Apparently Beethoven played for Goethe, after which the great author confessed himself deeply moved. Far from being gratified, Beethoven turned on him:

Oh Sir, I didn't expect this of you. In Berlin too, I was giving a concert some years ago. I made a great effort and thought I was giving a really good performance, and I hoped for some decent applause. But lo and behold! When I had expressed my utmost enthusiasm, not the faintest sound of applause was to be heard. That really was too much for me: I couldn't understand. However, the enigma soon resolved itself in this way: the whole Berlin public was so educated and refined that they now staggered towards me with their handkerchiefs wet with emotion to assure me of their gratitude. This was all quite irrelevant to a crude enthusiast like myself: I could see that I had only a romantic audience, not an artistic one. But from you, Goethe, I won't stand for this . . . You yourself must know how pleasant it is to be applauded by hands which one respects: if you don't recognize me and consider me as your equal, who will? To what sort of a pack of ragamuffins shall I turn for understanding?

The author of this account was Bettina Brentano, an exceptionally lively and imaginative young woman who was the half-sister of Beethoven's friend Franz Brentano. She was the main agent in getting Goethe and Beethoven together for that first meeting. For a while Beethoven and Bettina were on close terms.

♦

His relationship with Franz's wife Antonie, however, was closer still. It seems to have ripened during Antonie's long illness in 1811, when Beethoven often visited her and improvised for her. She arrived at Karlsbad while Beethoven was still in Teplitz in the summer of 1812, and it was then that another important Beethoven document was written – the letter to the person now described as 'The Immortal' or 'Eternally Beloved':

July 6th, in the morning

My angel, my all, my other self. – Only a few words today, and, what is more, written in pencil (and with your pencil) – I shan't be certain of my rooms here until tomorrow; what an unnecessary waste of time all this is – Why this profound sorrow, when necessity speaks – can our love endure without sacrifices, without our demanding everything from one another; can you alter the fact that you are not wholly mine, that I am not wholly yours? – Dear God, look at Nature in all her beauty and set your heart at rest about what must be – Love demands all, and rightly so, and thus it is for me with you, for you with me *– But you forget so easily that I must live* for me and for you; *if we were completely united, you would feel this painful necessity just as little as I do – My journey was dreadful and I did not arrive here until yesterday at four o'clock in the morning. As there were few horses the mailcoach chose another route, but what a dreadful road it was; at the last stage but one I was warned not to travel by night; attempts were made to frighten me about a forest, but all this only spurred me on to proceed – and it was wrong of me to do so. The coach broke down, of course, owing to the dreadful road which had not been made up and was nothing but a country track. If I hadn't had those two postillions I would have been left stranded on the way – On the other ordinary road Esterházy with eight horses met with the same fate as I did with four – Yet I feel to a certain extent the pleasure I always feel when I have overcome some difficulty successfully – Well, let me turn quickly from outer to inner experiences. No doubt we shall meet soon; and today also time fails me to tell you of the thoughts which during these last few days I have been revolving about my life – If our hearts were always closely united, I would certainly entertain no such thoughts. My heart overflows with a longing to tell you so many things – Oh – there are moments when I find that speech is quite inadequate – Be cheerful – and be for ever my faithful, my only sweetheart, my all, as I am yours. The gods must send us everything else, whatever must and shall be our fate –*
Your faithful
Ludwig

Monday evening, July 6th

You are suffering, you, my most precious one – I have noticed this very moment that letters have to be handed in very early, on Monday – or on Thursday – the only days when the mail coach goes from here to K. – You are suffering – Oh, where I am, you are with me – I will see to it that you and I, that I can live with you. What a life!!!! as it is now!!! without you – pursued by the kindness of people here and there, a kindness that I think – that I wish to deserve just as little as I deserve it – man's homage to man – that pains me – and when I consider myself in the setting of the universe, what I am and what is that man – whom one calls the greatest of men – and yet – on the other hand therein lies the divine element in man – I weep when I think that probably you will not receive the first news of me until Saturday – However much you love me – my love for you is even greater – but never conceal yourself from me – good night! – Since I am taking the baths I must get off to sleep – Dear God – so near! so far! Is not our love truly founded in heaven – and, what is more, as strongly cemented as the firmament of Heaven? –

◆

Good morning, on July 7th
Even when I am in bed my thoughts rush to you, my eternally
beloved, now and then joyfully, then again sadly, waiting to
know whether fate will hear our prayer – To face life I must
live altogether with you or never see you. Yes, I am resolved
to be a wanderer abroad until I can fly to your arms and
say that I have found my true home with you and enfolded
in your arms can let my soul be wafted to the realm of the
blessed spirits – alas, unfortunately it must be so – You will
become composed, the more so as you know that I am faithful
to you; no other woman can ever possess my heart – never
– never – Oh God, why must one be separated from her who
is so dear. Yet my life in V. at present is a miserable life, –
Your love has made me both the happiest and the unhappiest
of mortals – At my age I now need stability and regularity
in my life – can this coexist with our relationship? – Angel,
I have just heard that the post goes every day – and therefore
I must close, so that you may receive the letter immediately
– Be calm; for only by calmly considering our lives can we
achieve our purpose to live together – Be calm – love me –
Today – yesterday – what tearful longing for you – for you
– you – my life – my all – all good wishes to you – Oh, do
continue to love me – never misjudge your lover's most faithful
heart.

ever yours
ever mine   L.
ever ours

♦

Like the Heiligenstadt Testament, this letter, too, was never sent – at least not in this form – but most scholars agree that it was almost certainly meant for Antonie Brentano.

Antonie is not the only contender for the title 'Immortal Beloved'. There is the Countess Josephine Deym, to whom Beethoven had written passionate letters in the mid 1800s. The song 'An die Hoffnung' ('To Hope') Op.32 was written for her in 1805, although two years later their relationship seems to have cooled.

Another, more likely candidate was Therese von Malfatti, niece of a musical physician friend, to whom Beethoven probably proposed in 1810. It seems that her family opposed the marriage, which would explain why Beethoven broke off relations with them at about this time.

But Therese was not in Karlsbad in July 1812; Antonie was. We shall probably never know how close the couple were. One thing is striking however: Beethoven did seem to have a capacity for falling for unattainable women. Antonie was married; other 'beloveds' were too obviously his social superiors. Perhaps, in his innermost heart, Beethoven preferred it that way.

There is evidence though that Beethoven may not have been completely celibate – that he was open to the possibility of the occasional 'dalliance'. His pupil Ferdinand Ries remembers turning up for a lesson and finding the composer with . . .

> . . . a handsome woman sitting beside him on the sofa. Feeling that I had come at an inopportune moment, I wanted to leave immediately, but Beethoven detained me and said: 'Sit down and play for a while!' He and the lady remained seated behind me. I had been playing for a long time when Beethoven suddenly called out: 'Ries! Play something romantic! Soon after: 'Something melancholy!' Then, 'Something passionate!' and so on.

Ries is unable to tell us whether this unusual seduction attempt was ultimately successful. But there is a telling entry in one of Beethoven's notebooks from 1817: 'Sensual enjoyment without the union of souls is and always will be bestial: after it there is no trace of exalted sentiment, rather one feels remorse.' This does seem to suggest that Beethoven knew from experience what that 'remorse' was like.

Whatever the case, his sense of isolation, and that lifelong tendency to look inward were to deepen in the years that followed. This, like his earlier struggles with 'fate', was to leave its mark on his music.

CRISIS
(1813–17)

The year of 1812, when the 'Immortal Beloved' letter was written, was one of the key dates in European history. It was then that Napoleon made his disastrous attempt to capture Moscow, drastically weakening his military resources in the process. Major defeats followed: Wellington won the Battle of Vittoria in June 1813, and the decisive victory of the combined Austrian, Russian and Prussian armies came at the Battle of the Nations in October. News of Wellington's triumph was greeted ecstatically in Vienna. Beethoven was persuaded to write a large-scale celebratory piece and the result was *Wellington's Victory* Op.91. It is not one of his greatest compositions, but its vivid depiction of the battling French and British armies (with '*God save the King*' triumphant at the end) is rousing, entertaining and not too demanding. The premiere, in December 1813, was one of the greatest successes of Beethoven's career.

Beethoven himself conducted one early performance of *Wellington's Victory*. The famous tenor Franz Wild saw him and remembered how he . . .

> . . . *provided a spectacle which staggered the senses. In the* piano *he sank to his knees, at the* forte *reached upwards so that, like a dwarf, he would vanish altogether under the conductor's stand, then, like a giant, he would tower above it. All the while his arms and hands would be in motion as*

if with the music a thousand lives had taken possession of his every limb. At the beginning this did not endanger the effect of the work. He became invisible at the forte *passages and reappeared at the* piano *passages. Danger now threatened, and at the decisive moment Kapellmeister Umlauf took command, making it clear to the orchestra that they should follow him. For a long time Beethoven did not notice anything. When at last he became aware of it, there came to his lips a smile which, if ever it had been my good fortune to see one, deserves the appellation 'heavenly'.*

The audience evidently agreed with Beethoven, and they roared their approval.

The arrival of about 10,000 foreign visitors for the Congress of Vienna in 1814 and 1815 created a carnival-like atmosphere in the Austrian capital. Representatives of all the victorious powers met to decide how Europe should be divided up after Napoleon's defeat. Naturally, France was to be punished: the Congress deprived the vanquished French republic of its conquests and forced it to pay huge compensations. The presiding genius was the Austrian Foreign Minister, Prince Klemens von Metternich who, vain but with an instinct for good publicity, rapidly became the figurehead of the new conservativism. His call to European leaders to cooperate in the fight against democratization and liberalism was well received.

Ironically, the democratic liberal Beethoven was to become another hero of the hour. While the successes of *Wellington's Victory* and of the newly-premiered *Seventh* and *Eighth Symphonies* Opp.92 & 93 still reverberated, it was suggested that his failed liberation-opera *Leonore* should be revived. So it was, in 1814, though only after Beethoven had revised it again and (rather reluctantly) allowed the title to be changed. Today the opera, Op.72, is known by that second title, *Fidelio*, although Beethoven always said that he preferred the original. As *Fidelio* the opera was so successful that a performance was arranged for some of the foreign heads of state assembled for the Congress. One wonders what the reactionary Metternich might have made of it, particularly of the portrayal of the tyrannical prison governor, Don Pizzaro.

The climate, however, was soon to change. Post-war euphoria

was quickly followed by depression, economically and spiritually. Suddenly there was far less money in circulation, and some of Beethoven's aristocratic friends were among the chief sufferers. Count Razumovsky, for instance, lost heavily, and was unable to repair his sumptuous palace after a fire in 1814. He disbanded his famous string quartet soon afterwards and its leader, Ignaz Schuppanzigh, left to try his fortunes in Russia. Two of Beethoven's important patrons died: Prince Lichnowsky in 1814, and Prince Lobkowitz in 1816.

And almost as suddenly, the Viennese found a new musical hero, the Italian operatic composer Gioachino Rossini. A report to the secret police, filed the day after the first performance of the cantata '*Der glorreiche Augenblick*' ('The Glorious Moment'), notes, with apparent satisfaction, that:

> *Yesterday's musical Academy did not in any way increase esteem for the talent of H. Beethoven. There are factions pro and contra Beethoven. In contrast to Razumowsky, Apponyi, Kraft, who deify Beethoven, there exists a substantial majority of knowledgeable people who want to hear no music whatsoever by Herr Beethoven.*

The notebooks and diaries of the time suggest that the change in Beethoven's standing, and in the mood of the times, may have forced him to look deeper into himself and to examine his beliefs. Here are some comments scribbled down during the year 1815:

> *All that is called life shall be sacrificed to sublime Art, a sacrament of Art! Let me live, even by means of artificial aide! if only such are to be found!*

> *If possible, develop the ear instruments, then travel! This you owe to yourself, to men and to Him, the Almighty: only in this way may you be able to develop once more all that has remained latent within you. And a small Court, a small Chapel, the song of praise written in it by me, performed, to the glory of the Almighty, the Eternal, the Infinite! Thus may my last days pass – and for future humanity! Händel, Bach, Gluck, Mozart, Haydn's portraits in my room, they can help me to deserve indulgence.*

> *Almighty in the forest! I am happy, blissful in the forest: every tree speaks through you. Oh God! what splendour! In such a wooded scene, on the heights there is calm, calm in which to serve Him.*

But to most members of the Viennese musical world it must have looked as though Beethoven had simply had his day. The great musical outpouring of the decade after Heiligenstadt had all but ceased. New works now appeared rarely and at very irregular intervals. Beethoven gave his last public performance in May 1814, playing the piano part in the '*Archduke*' *Piano Trio*. It was embarrassing. Another composer, Ludwig Spohr, described it as follows:

> *On account of his deafness there was scarcely anything left of the virtuosity that had formerly been so greatly admired. In* forte *passages the poor man pounded on the keys till the strings jangled, and in* piano *he played so softly that whole groups of notes were omitted, so that the music was incomprehensible.*

As his hearing deteriorated further, he seemed to care less and less about his appearance, or about his living conditions. The Baron de Trémont described Beethoven's lodgings thus:

> *Picture to yourself the dirtiest, most disorderly place imaginable – patches of moisture all over the ceiling, an oldish grand piano, on which dust contended with various pieces of engraved and manuscript music; under the piano (I do not exaggerate) an unemptied* pot de nuit. . . . *The chairs, most of them with cane seats, were covered with plates bearing the remains of last night's dinner and clothes etc.*

Beethoven grumbled continually about Vienna. A Dr. Carl von Bursy met him in June 1816 and heard from him how the city was 'mean and dirty. Things could not be worse. From top to bottom everything is shabby. You can't trust anyone. What is not written down in black and white, no one will honour. They want your work and then pay you a beggar's pittance, not even what they agreed to pay. . . .' And yet he continued to stay, despite signs of continuing interest in him from other countries. Irritating as the city was, he seems to have needed it. Perhaps that very irritation was a stimulus, as it seems to have been, nearly a century later, for another great composer, Gustav Mahler.

For the moment, though, Beethoven was preoccupied with a new, non-musical problem. In November 1815, Beethoven's brother Caspar Carl died of consumption. He left a widow, Johanna, and a son, Karl. Not long before he died, Caspar Carl had persuaded Beethoven to accept the joint guardianship of Karl, with Johanna, in the event of his death, even though he knew Beethoven and Johanna disliked each other. The closing words of his will are a triumph of hope over experience: 'I recommend *compliance* to my wife and more *moderation* to my brother.' Moderation? – *Beethoven?*

Whatever his initial reaction, Beethoven's feelings had soon turned to a passionate, possessive love. It was as though the nine-year-old Karl were his own son. He ignored the conditions of the will and began a long legal campaign to prove that Johanna was unfit to look after the boy. In January 1816, the court, rather surprisingly, decided in Beethoven's favour and he was appointed sole guardian.

If it had not occurred to him already, Beethoven soon realized that he was in no position to offer Karl a proper home, and so he set about looking for a boarding school – somewhere as far away from Johanna as possible. But even when Karl was safely dispatched, his protectiveness and his hatred of Johanna continued to grow. 'I have fought a battle to wrest a poor unhappy child from the clutches of his unworthy mother, and I have won', he wrote to Antonie Brentano. 'He is the source of many cares, but *cares that are sweet to me.*' His imagination ran riot: Johanna had offered herself 'for hire' to men; she had poisoned her husband. Before long he was referring to her in his letters as the Queen of the Night, after the spectacular evil sorceress in Mozart's opera *The Magic Flute.*

Eventually Beethoven could no longer bear to have Karl out of his immediate protection. He took the boy back under his own roof in January 1818, giving the school strict instructions not to tell Johanna. Meanwhile, Johanna made two more attempts to get her son back, both unsuccessful. The effect of all this on Karl can only be imagined. One private tutor engaged by Beethoven refused to teach Karl after he heard him pouring out abuse against Johanna – no doubt encouraged by Beethoven. But then, in December 1818, Karl suddenly fled to his mother. The police found him and returned him to Beethoven, but Johanna was able to use Karl's attempted escape as an excuse to file another petition in the court.

What happened next will seem extraordinary to modern readers, but it underlines the differences between the social order in Beethoven's time and in our own. So far the applications had been heard in the Landrecht, where those of noble birth were legally represented. But in the middle of this latest case, Beethoven said of Karl, in passing, 'Of course, if he were of noble birth . . . ' and it was thus revealed to the court that Beethoven had no right to be there – it seems that up till then he had been able to use the *van/von* confusion to his advantage. Beethoven attempted to justify his position with remarks about nobility of heart and mind, but it was no use. The case was transfered to the commoners' court – to Beethoven's mortification – and this time he lost. Johanna now did her best to get Karl out of the country, but that required permission from the authorities, and they refused. In desperation Beethoven appealed, this time with the help of some of his powerful friends, notably the Archduke Rudolph. With such names behind him, the court was inclined to see his case differently and, in April 1820, the decision went for him and against Johanna. The one course left to Johanna was a direct appeal to the Emperor. She tried, but failed, and on 24 July 1820 the case was declared closed.

Beethoven had won, legally speaking, but the cost in human terms was high. The emotional turmoil and constantly changing fortunes took an enormous amount out of him; his health suffered frequently during this four-and-a-half-year struggle. And the effect on Karl was profoundly destabilizing. In his heart, Beethoven must have had his doubts about the wisdom of it all. He even showed signs of compassion for the Queen of the Night: 'It pains me to have to make someone suffer through my good works for my dear Karl!!!'

As far as compositions went during this period, with the exception of the *Leonore–Fidelio* revision, the works that appeared after *Wellington's Victory* were not, on the whole, impressive. The tender, intimate *Piano Sonata* Op.90 No.27 (1814) was an exception, but how strongly it contrasts with such empty exercises as the Overture *Namensfeier* Op.115 (for the name-day of the Kaiser) or the cantata '*The Glorious Moment*' Op.136, both from the same year. An opera was contemplated, on the legend of Romulus and Remus, founders of ancient Rome, but it came to nothing. A *Sixth Piano Concerto* (1815) and a *Piano Trio in F minor* (1816) got somewhat further, but they too were eventually abandoned.

Good, lasting work is rare in those years. The two *Cello Sonatas* Op.102 appeared in 1815 and in 1816 Beethoven wrote a song cycle, *An die ferne Geliebte* ('To the distant beloved') Op.98, which was an interesting title given Beethoven's recurring attraction to unattainable women. And while he was at work on *An die ferne Geliebte*, Beethoven began one of his finest piano sonatas to date, Op.101 No.28 in A major, written for the Baroness Dorothea Ertmann. A coincidence? Dorothea, who had been one of Beethoven's pupils, was one of the outstanding Beethoven pianists of her day. She was attractive, and married, and Beethoven was at least fond of her. He nicknamed her 'Dorothea Cäcilia', the second name after Cecilia, the patron saint of music.

There is a very touching story of how Beethoven helped her come to terms with the loss of her first child. According to the actress Antonie von Arneth, 'after the funeral of her only child she could not find tears. General Ertmann brought her to Beethoven. The Master spoke no words but played for her until she began to sob, so her sorrow found an outlet and comfort.'

These four works are each, in their very different ways, vintage Beethoven, and the Op.101 *Piano Sonata* and the second of the Cello Sonatas Op.102 are often seen as forerunners of Beethoven's 'late' style, in which the contemplative, spiritual side of his musical personality takes over increasingly from earlier attempts to 'take fate by the throat'. The monumental '*Hammerklavier*' *Sonata*, Op.106 No.29, composed in the year after Op.101, seems like a summary of his musical development at this stage. In many ways it is to the piano sonata what the '*Eroica*' is to the symphony. But if this is a 'heroic' work, it is heroism of a new kind. After the titanic struggles of the first movement and the disruptive, fantastic Scherzo, the slow movement probes new depths of inner darkness – it is perhaps the most agonizingly soul-searching music Beethoven ever wrote. Could it be that this movement represents a working out of feelings about the Karl crisis? After this a massive, fugal Finale rises from the ashes, making dramatic use of the extended keyboard of the new make of piano, or 'Hammerklavier' as Beethoven liked to call it; and yet one of the most memorable passages is a moment of calm, with a simple fugal theme in even, flowing crotchets. This is more than a prophecy of the 'late' Beethoven; we are already there.

All of this is magnificent music, but five fine works in four years hardly compares with the mighty outpouring of the post-Heiligenstadt years. But creative thought isn't always what it seems. While the conscious mind is relatively inactive, or preoccupied with day-to-day things, the unconscious can be doing its own work, and that may well have been the case with Beethoven. Two important musical seeds were sown during the years when he was fighting for Karl. In June 1817 the Philharmonic Society of London sent him a letter, inviting him to visit London the following winter and to compose two new symphonies, for a fee of 300 guineas. The idea of going to London appealed to him strongly. After Wellington's defeat of Napoleon he had replaced his one-time French republican sympathies with an admiration for British parliamentary democracy. He had even made arrangements of folk songs from the British Isles Op.108, as an expression of 'a certain very particular regard and affection I feel for the English nation and also for Scottish melody.' Soon afterwards sketches began to appear for one of the new symphonies.

The second important stimulus was the news that his old and close friend the Archduke Rudolph was to be appointed Archbishop of Olmütz (now Olumouc in the Czech republic). Beethoven was soon sketching a *Missa Solemnis* ('solemn mass') for Rudolph's enthronement in 1820. He seems to have taken this as cue to re-examine his own religious beliefs. Beethoven was not an orthodox Catholic. He believed in an all-powerful divine being, whom he sometimes addressed as 'Father', but his idea of God also owed something to non-Christian philosophers and religious writers. Christ, for him, was a figure comparable with the ancient Greek philosopher Socrates, who had similarly been martyred for his teachings. In his diary, he noted down sentences from the Hindu *Rig-Veda* scriptures: 'Free from all passion and desire, that is the Mighty One. He is alone. None is greater than He.' Three lines from ancient Egyptian texts were copied out neatly and kept, framed, on his desk:

I am that which is.

I am all – what is, what was, what will be; no mortal man has ever lifted my veil.

He is only and solely of Himself and to this only One all things owe their existence.

At the same time Beethoven began to do what few composers before him had done: to make a thorough study of religious music of the past. In these days of bulging record catalogues, when music from almost every age is available at the press of a compact disc player start-button, we can easily forget that in Beethoven's time the musical past was the recent past. J.S. Bach (1685–1750) was only just beginning to be widely rediscovered, although Beethoven had grown up with his works, and the oratorios of Bach's contemporary Handel had long been familiar territory. But he also looked beyond, to the music of the great Renaissance church composer Palestrina, to older writings on setting religious texts, and to unaccompanied liturgical chant, or 'plainsong', which he found increasingly inspiring.

As it turned out, neither the mass nor the first of the two London-commissioned symphonies was to be ready in time. The gestation period took far longer than Beethoven expected. But this is hardly surprising: the *Missa Solemnis* Op.123 and the *Ninth Symphony* Op.125 were to be grander, more complex and at the same time more profoundly personal than anything he had written before. And the works that were to appear in their wake were to radiate a new sense of self-discovery, and in the process to set a remarkable seal on an already remarkable musical career.

CHAPTER 5
THE 'LATE' PERIOD
(1820–27)

♦ *Deteriorating health*
♦ *Missa Solemnis and Ninth Symphony*
♦ *Last days*

The final decision of the Court of Appeal concerning Karl removed a huge burden from Beethoven's shoulders. The effect seems to have been an immediate release of creative energy. In April 1820, just after the Court ruling, he began to work again on the *Missa Solemnis*. Up until then he had only sketched the Gloria and the Credo; now he turned his attention to the other movements, and he may have finished the complete sketch as early as October. Then, in May, a commission came from a German publisher for three piano sonatas.

Beethoven started the first of these, Op.109, at once, but it was to take him two years to finish them. The problem was not lack of inspiration, but worsening health. Beethoven spent six weeks in bed with rheumatic fever in early 1821, and during July and August he was struck with jaundice. And yet he continued to struggle with his ideas for the sonatas and the *Missa Solemnis*, even though the deadline for the latter was well past. In the meantime, he managed to compose five *Bagatelles* (Op.119 Nos.7–11). These are fascinating little pieces, which may look light and inconsequential at first, but which turn out to be full of surprises. The final piece, No.11 in B flat, is a lovely, intimate miniature, with a hint of the other-worldly humour of the last piano sonatas.

But it is in those three *Sonatas*, Op.109 No.30 *in E*, Op.110 No.31 *in A flat*, and Op.111 No.32 *in C minor*, that we find the sustained greatness typical of the 'late' Beethoven. Op.109 concludes with a breathtakingly inventive set of variations on a simple but eloquent theme. The theme returns at the end, unchanged except for the removal of the original repeats, and yet in spirit it seems utterly transformed. Op.110 similarly follows two short movements with a much longer one, although here the Finale is cast in a unique song-plus-fugue form. Two statements of the lamenting song-theme – the second in broken phrases, as though heavy with grief – alternate with aspiring fugal sections, later marked *Nach und nach wieder auflebend* – 'little by little returning to life'.

Op.111 is generally held to be the finest of the three. In the fast first movement Beethoven returns for the last time to the heroic C minor mode, only this time the struggle ends neither in tragedy nor in noisy victory, but with a wonderfully warm, pianissimo C major chord. After this comes a series of variations in the major key, contemplative, wildly dancing, and finally reaching an ecstatic calm. It is a marvellous end to a great sonata cycle, although there was still more piano music to come: another set of *Bagatelles* Op.126 (1824) and one last serious work, the immense *Diabelli Variations*, Op.120.

The composer Anton Diabelli had sent his theme to some fifty composers, including Beethoven, as early as 1819, with a request that each composer should write one variation on it. It was a very plain little waltz with no tune to speak of, and when Beethoven saw it for the first time he was unenthusiastic – it was, he said, nothing better than a *Schusterfleck*, a 'cobbler's patch'. But tunes that are beautiful or striking in their own right are not always the best basis for variations, and before long Diabelli's scrap of a theme had begun to fascinate Beethoven.

In the end he produced not one, but thirty-three variations on it. Bach's extended *Goldberg Variations* may have been a model, but the *Diabelli Variations* remain pure Beethoven, full of joy, mystery, lamentation and a kind of titanic humour. The climactic fugal variation (No.32) brings the work to a crisis: key, pulse, theme – all seem momentarily to dissolve; but then Diabelli's waltz returns, transformed into a graceful, ornate minuet. Order is resumed, but with a smile.

The *Diabelli Variations* were finished in 1823. The same year saw the long-awaited completion of the *Missa Solemnis*. One hopes that when the Archduke heard it, he understood why it had taken so long. The *Missa Solemnis* is a unique musical achievement. There are echoes of the formalized eighteenth-century mass, but the overall conception is on a completely different plane. The sweet worldliness of the rococo chapel is gone and in its place an awesome cathedral, which, like the magnificent gothic interior of St Stephen's, Vienna, seems to draw together elements from many different ages.

In some parts of the *Missa Solemnis* Beethoven's struggles have left their mark on the fabric of the music. Anton Schindler, one of the composer's first biographers, remembered going to visit the composer while he was working on the Credo.

> *In one of the living-rooms, behind closed doors, we heard the master singing, howling and stamping his foot to the Credo fugue. We had listened for some time to this dreadful noise and were on the point of leaving, when the doors opened and Beethoven stood before us, his face so distorted as to fill one with alarm. He looked as though he had just survived a life-and-death struggle with a whole host of contrapuntalists.*

Parts of the fugue in question – at the words *et vitam venturi saeculi* ('and the life of the world to come') – sound as if they could only have been written that way; and yet how typical of the older Beethoven to end this monumental movement peacefully, with gently running scales for woodwind and strings.

Alongside the craggy counterpoint are moments of incomparable serenity: the *Et incarnatus*, with its almost improvisatory flute writing, and the *Benedictus* show that the unorthodox Beethoven could still be touched by the great Catholic symbols, the incarnation of Christ and the celebration of his sacrifice in the blessed sacrament. In the final *Agnus dei* something quite different happens: the horror of the still-recent European war invades the music in the form of threatening trumpet and drum fanfares.

After this the soprano's anguished cries for peace are all the more stirring. In composing this Beethoven must have remembered the bombardment of 1809, and perhaps also his own near-encounter with the French forces on his way from Bonn to Vienna in 1792. It adds special urgency to the famous inscription on the title page: 'From the heart – may it go again to the heart!'

The other large-scale project, the *Ninth Symphony*, progressed more steadily once the *Missa Solemnis* was out of the way. It was finally finished in February 1824, by which time Beethoven had departed some way from his original plans.

Originally the *Ninth* was to have been a purely orchestral work, like the previous eight, with a Finale in the home key of D minor. But, at some stage during composition, Beethoven was struck by a bold idea. For many years he had considered making a choral and orchestral setting of the poem *Ode to Joy* by the German poet, playwright and historian Johann Friedrich von Schiller. Might this not make an excellent Finale for the new symphony? No one had ever included voices in a symphony before, but that was unlikely to deter Beethoven. The original Finale theme was put aside (he later used it in the *A minor String Quartet*, Op.132 No.15), to be replaced by an improved version of the theme from the *Choral Fantasia* of 1808.

The symphony is on the same huge scale as the *Missa Solemnis*. First comes a sweeping, tragic opening movement, followed by an elemental Scherzo (a 'cosmic dance' was one writer's description) and a tender, heartfelt slow movement. So far, although the length of the movements is unprecedented, the formal design is broadly familiar. But now Beethoven breaks into completely new territory.

A violent, convulsive fanfare is answered by recitatives for cellos and double basses, punctuated by reminiscences of the three previous movements. Then comes the new 'joy' theme, elegantly and powerfully varied by the orchestra. At its height, the strident fanfare returns, to be answered not by orchestral basses, but by a human bass voice – 'Oh friends, not these sounds!' – and then, as though in response to his words, the chorus itself takes up the 'joy' theme.

It is easy to see why Schiller's poem inspired Beethoven. The image of God is one that he would have found very sympathetic: 'Brothers, above the canopy of stars, there must dwell a dear Father.'

But the poem is as much about human beings as it is about God – 'All men will be brothers.' The music underlines that idea vividly. After an awe-inspiring climax at the words 'And the cherub stands before God', there is a moment's silence before the bassoons, double bassoon, bass drum and later triangle and cymbals lead off in a cheeky, march-like version of the 'joy' theme. The message is clear: at this point popular music marches off the streets and into the concert hall. 'All men' really means all men, not just the aristocracy or the rising bourgeoisie.

When news of the Ninth Symphony's completion began to spread, there were anxious discussions. Would Beethoven entrust the first performance to London? Would he accept an offer from Berlin to have the symphony and the *Missa Solemnis* premiered there? A petition was presented to Beethoven, urgently requesting him to stage the first performances in Vienna. It came too late to prevent the premiere of the *Missa Solemnis* in St Petersburg, but the Kärntnertor Theatre was booked for the first performance of the symphony. As usual, Beethoven insisted on his own conditions: the violinist Ignaz Schuppanzig, newly returned from Russia, had to lead the orchestra, there had to be sufficient time for rehearsal. But the date for the first performance was agreed: 7 May.

On the evening of the concert, the theatre – with the notable exception of the imperial box – was packed with people. The audience was unusually attentive, and at one point in the Scherzo – where drums thunder out a repeated figure – parts of the crowd broke into spontaneous applause. At the end the cheering and clapping was thunderous, although Beethoven, standing facing the orchestra in front of the conductor's desk, was completely unaware of it until the contralto soloist, Caroline Unger, turned him round. If he was moved by what he saw, he didn't show it.

This impassiveness – or as one witness interpreted it, 'ungraciousness' – may simply have been a reflection of how much Beethoven had withdrawn in recent years. He was now completely deaf, and communication was carried on almost exclusively through the so-called 'Conversation Books', in which those who wished to speak with Beethoven wrote down their questions or observations. Sometimes all we have are the questions addressed to Beethoven – presumably he spoke his replies: but the gaps on paper can be very telling. This is Gerhard von Breuning, son of Beethoven's old friend Stephan, on the subject of the composer's amanuensis, Carl Holz, in 1827:

> *No one can stand Holz; for everyone who knows him says he's treacherous. He pretends that he likes you ever so much.*

He's very good at deceiving.

He can lie like a book.

You're the best of them all, the others are scoundrels.

If you weren't so kind-hearted, you'd have the right to ask him to pay for his board.

He likes your wine best of all.

At other times some of Beethoven's responses were written too, as in these pages from 1823. This time he is talking to Anton Schindler in 1823 about Giulietta Guicciardi, to whom he had dedicated the '*Moonlight*' *Sonata*, twelve years earlier. It seems the topic was still a sensitive one.

[Beethoven] I was very much loved by her, far more than her husband ever was – he was really more her lover than I was. But from her I heard about his poverty and I found a rich man who gave me 500 florins to help him out.

He was always my enemy and that is the reason why I did him all the good that I could.

[Schindler] Where upon he said to me, 'He is an intolerable man', undoubtably out of sheer gratitude. But, Father, forgive them, for they know not what they do! . . .

It is a long time since she was married to Mons. de Gallenberg?

[Beethoven] She was born Guicciardi.

She was already his wife before [she went to Italy], and she came to see me in tears but I spurned her.

Hercules at the crossroads.

If I had wanted to spend my strength and my life in this manner, what would have been left over for the nobler better part?

The reference to wine in the first extract may have been a little pointed. By the mid 1820s Beethoven was drinking heavily – a bottle of wine per meal according to one report – and he could be spectacularly neglectful of his appearance.

Gerhard von Breuning, whom we have just met in the first Conversation Book example, was a regular visitor to the composer's lodgings during the years 1825 to 1827. He recollected:

Beethoven's outward appearance, due to his peculiar casualness in the matter of dress, had something uncommonly conspicuous about it in the street. Usually lost in thought and humming to himself, he would often wave his arms about when walking alone. When in company, his speech would be lively and loud, and, as his companion would then have to write his reply in the conversation book, an abrupt halt would have to be made; this was conspicuous enough in itself, and still more so if the reply had to be communicated in mime.

So it happened that most passers-by would turn around to stare at him; street urchins mocked and shouted at him. For that reason his nephew Karl refused to go out with him and once told him straight out that he was ashamed to accompany him in the street because of his 'comical appearance'; at this, he told us, he was terribly offended and hurt. For my part, I was proud to show myself with a man of such importance.

The crown of the felt hat he wore then had lost its shape and bulged towards the top where it had been stretched; this was the result of Beethoven's habit, on coming in, of thrusting his hat onto the top point of the hat-stand; should the hat be dripping with rain, he would simply shake it a little first, which he did at our house without a thought for the furniture. The hat was rarely if ever brushed, either before or after the rain, and becoming increasingly dusty, it took on a permanently matted appearance. He wore it, when possible, at the back of his head to have his forehead free, while his grey, uncombed hair . . . flew out on both sides. . . . I often saw him thus from our windows, if I was not with him myself, coming at about two o'clock – his lunch hour – from the Schottentor across the part of the Glacis where the Votivkirche now stands, sailing towards his apartment at his usual posture, his body thrust forward (but not bowed), his head erect.

At about this time we read of Beethoven being mistaken for a tramp and arrested. It is not hard to believe, nor is it hard to imagine his reaction. And yet this same man was on the verge of what many believe to be his finest achievement, the last five string quartets.

It was the Russian Prince Nikolai Galitsin, conductor at the St Petersburg premiere of the *Missa Solemnis*, who planted in Beethoven's mind the suggestion that he might write another set of quartets. He finished the *First*, Op.127 No.12 *in E flat*, in January 1825. In many ways it is the culmination of the lyrical side of Beethoven's musical character, especially the slow second movement, a set of variations on one of his loveliest song-themes. Next comes Op.132 No.15 *in A minor* – dark, troubled, but with a radiant slow movement subtitled '*Hymn of thanksgiving to the Deity, from a convalescent*', the rapt 'Hymn' section alternating with a bright, dancing passage marked 'feeling new strength'.

The next *Quartet*, Op.130 No.13 *in B flat* (the official numbering is slightly misleading here), is rather like a baroque multi-movement suite. The *Große Fuge* (Grand Fugue), Op.133 was the quartet's original Finale, and certainly makes an uplifting conclusion. But before it comes a movement called 'Cavatina', a song of profound sadness with, at its heart, a halting violin passage marked *Beklemmt* – 'oppressed'. Beethoven's secretary at this time, Karl Holz, recalled that it was the composer's 'favourite piece. . . . In fact he composed it in tears of melancholy (during the summer of 1825) and he confessed to me that his own music had never had such an effect on him before, and that even thinking back to that piece cost him fresh tears.'

But the quartet that Beethoven thought the greatest of them all was the *C sharp minor Quartet*, Op.131 No.14. Its form is utterly original – it is hard, for instance, to say whether it is in five movements or seven. In a good performance the effect can be like an impassioned spiritual journey, one great, continually unfolding movement with many different facets.

The slow section before the Finale is another heart-breaking instrumental song, and this time there may have been a direct cause in Beethoven's personal life. In 1826 his nephew Karl, driven almost to distraction by Beethoven's eccentricity and suffocating possessiveness, tried to shoot himself. He failed, but his injuries required long treatment. Beethoven seems to have realized at last that he had to let Karl go, and with the help of Stephan van Breuning (now a councillor in the war department) Karl obtained an army post, finally leaving Beethoven at the beginning of 1827. The dedication of the *C sharp minor Quartet* to Baron Joseph von Stutterheim is surely significant – von Stutterheim was the commander of the army regiment that Karl was to join.

But the final *Quartet*, Op.135 No.16 *in F*, seems to point in new directions. It is more modest, more 'classical' in scale, and although the slow movement is as deeply confessional as anything else in these last quartets, the Finale is full of delightful, humorous touches, nowhere more so than at the beginning, where an ominous questioning figure (marked with the words 'Must it be? It must be!') suddenly receives a cheerful, almost irreverent reply. It is that cheerful 'reply' motif that ends this last quartet – as though with a light shrug of the shoulders.

There was one further completed piece, an alternative finale for Op.130. At the first performance some listeners had taken exception to the *Große Fuge*, and for once Beethoven bowed to criticism. Players, critics and Beethoven enthusiasts still argue about whether he was right to do so, and many performances reinstate the *Große Fuge* to its original position.

Having finished this last project, Beethoven found his health declining again. The jaundice returned, and with it came an attack of dropsy. There were consolations: the London Philharmonic Society sent him a very generous gift of £100, and others sent presents. From Johann Stumpff, the London-based harpist, came the new forty-volume edition of Handel's works, which Beethoven described as a 'glorious gift'.

In February he asked the publisher Schott to send him some Rhine or Mosel wine, the taste of which would probably still carry associations with his Rhineland childhood. He continued to make sketches for a new symphony, but work was becoming harder as his condition grew worse. There were operations, but it was becoming less and less likely that he would recover. Reluctantly, Beethoven agreed to receive the last rites on 22 March. Two days later, as his case of wine arrived, he remarked sadly, 'Pity, pity, too late.'

Shortly afterwards, he fell into a coma. He died on 26 March. The composer Anselm Hüttenbrenner was with him.

> *After 5 o'clock there was suddenly a terrific clap of thunder*
> *accompanied by a flash of lightning which filled the death-chamber*
> *with a harsh light. . . . After this unexpected natural occurrence,*
> *which shook me greatly, Beethoven opened his eyes, lifted his right*
> *hand and looked up for several seconds with his fist clenched*
> *and a very serious, threatening expression. . . . As he let his hand*
> *sink again to the bed, his eyes half closed. My right hand supported*
> *his head, my left hand rested on his breast. No more breath, no*
> *more heartbeat.*

The city of Vienna, which had feted, derided, ignored and mar-
velled at him during his lifetime, managed a magnificent tribute
after his death. There was a huge funeral: something of the order
of 20,000 people turned up to pay their last respects. No composer before Beethoven had ever been honoured like this. The
pianist-composer Johann Nepomuk Hummel helped carry the
coffin, and amongst the torch-bearers were Czerny, Schuppanzigh, the poet Franz Grillparzer and the thirty-year-old Franz
Schubert, then just over a year away from his own death. At the
gates of the cemetery, the actor Heinrich Anschütz, an acquain-
tance of Beethoven's in his last years, delivered a funeral oration
written by Grillparzer. The words show eloquently what this
difficult, contradictory, sometimes painfully unhappy man had by
then come to symbolize:

> *We who stand here at the grave of the deceased one are in a sense*
> *the representatives of a nation, the entire German people, some*
> *to mourn the passing of one celebrated part of that which remained*
> *to us from the vanished radiance of the art of our homeland, of*
> *the spiritual efflorescence of the fatherland. The hero of poetry*
> *in the German language [Goethe] still lives – and long may he*
> *live. But the last master of resounding song, the gracious medium*
> *through which music spoke, the man who inherited and magnified*
> *the immortal fame of Handel and Bach, of Haydn and Mozart,*
> *has ceased to be; and we stand weeping over the broken strings*
> *of an instrument now silenced. . . .*
>
> *An instrument now stilled. Allow me to call him that! For*
> *he was an artist, and what he was, he was only through art.*
> *The thorns of life had wounded him deeply, and as the ship-*
> *wrecked man strives for the redeeming shore, he flew into your*

arms, oh wondrous sister of the good and true, comforter in affliction, the art that comes from on high! . . . He was an artist, and who shall stand beside him? . . . he traversed all, he comprehended everything. He who follows him cannot continue; he must begin anew, for his predecessor ended only where art ends. . . .

He was an artist, but also a man, a man in every sense, in the highest sense. Because he turned away from the world, they called him hostile, and callous because he shunned feelings. Oh, he who knows he is hardened does not flee! . . . He withdrew from his fellow men after he had given them everything and had received nothing in return. . . . But in his death he kept a human heart for all men, a father's heart for his own people, the whole world.

Thus he was, thus he died, thus he will live for all time!

CHAPTER 6
BEETHOVEN
IN HISTORY

Beethoven's death is by no means the end of the story. As Grillparzer's funeral oration shows, the composer had begun to assume a mythological significance even in his own lifetime, and in the years that followed, he was to develop into one of the great symbolic figures of the Romantic movement – the type of the 'Artist Hero'. Volumes were written about him: not just biographies and critical commentaries, but poetry, Beethoven-philosophy and semi-fictional plays and novels.

Bettina Brentano – later Bettina von Arnim – who had helped stage-manage the meeting between Beethoven and Goethe in 1812, was an important contributor. Not only did she describe (and probably embroider) her own relationship with Beethoven; she attempted to define the basic qualities that gave his music its mysterious power. One of her disciples later summed these up under the headings 'The child of nature', 'The revolutionary', 'The magician' and 'The religious leader and prophet'.

The authenticity of Bettina's accounts of her friendship with Beethoven is controversial. Genuine or not, the following remarks, which she attributes to the composer, are typical of the kind of sentiments that were put into his mouth by literary admirers in the later nineteenth century:

> *When I open my eyes, I must sigh, for what I look upon is contrary to my religion, and I must despise the world which never divines that music is a greater revelation than the whole of wisdom and philosophy; music is the wine that incites us to new creation and I am the Bacchus who presses this glorious wine for mankind and grants them drunkenness of the spirit; when they are sober again they will have fished*

*up much which they may take with them on to dry land. I have
no friend, must live alone with myself; yet I know well that God
is nearer to me in my art than to others, I consort with Him
without fear, have always recognized and understood Him, nor
am I at all anxious about the fate of my music; its fate cannot
be other than happy; whoever succeeds in grasping it shall be
absolved from all the misery that bows down other men.*

The culmination of this form of Beethoven-worship came in
1902, when Vienna staged a huge Beethoven exhibition. Central
to this was a spectacular monument, by Max Klinger, made of
marble, ivory, precious stones, gold and bronze. Beethoven, semi-
naked, is seated in a classical heroic pose on a throne adorned
with angels' heads. The artist Gustav Klimt provided a frieze,
with mystical scenes supposedly depicting the essence of
Beethoven's achievement. For the opening ceremony the composer Gustav Mahler made a huge rearrangement of the *Ninth
Symphony*, with extra brass bands and massed choruses.

Two world wars and the death of the romantic art-religion
wrought great changes in people's understanding of Beethoven.
Ideologies of very different kinds claimed him as their own. After
the Russian Revolution, Beethoven became for some the model
of the 'revolutionary' artist. Later, Nazi Germany hailed him as a
great national artist, although Hitler was less enthusiastic about
Beethoven than he was about Richard Wagner, some of whose
views were rather closer to his own. Then, when the Germans
invaded France, the famous opening theme of the *Fifth Symphony*
– which spells the letter 'V' in morse code – became a symbol of
victory for the French Resistance.

Another reason for the change in understanding of
Beethoven was a shift in the relative evaluation of his works. The
romantics had focused on the works of the so-called 'heroic'
period, the decade after the 'Heiligenstadt Testament'. The late
works, however, with the exception of the *Ninth Symphony* were
appreciated by very few. The last five string quartets remained
'difficult' music until well into the twentieth century. The English critic John Ruskin would have spoken for many when, in 1881,
he wrote that the later Beethoven 'always sounds to me like the
upsetting of a bag of nails, with here and there an also dropped
hammer.' But in this century emphasis has shifted more and more

towards those last great works, partly through the influence of such outstandingly perceptive performers as the pianist Artur Schnabel and the members of the Busch Quartet. Their recordings, although made long before the age of stereo, are still regarded as classics.

Beethoven's influence on later composers has been colossal, inspiring, but often also inhibiting. For Schubert (1797–1828), Beethoven's death was part tragic loss and part liberation. His *String Quintet in C major*, long interpreted as a farewell to life, may be an attempt to pick up where Beethoven left off – Beethoven had left a fragment of a *Quintet in C* at his death, which Schubert saw in 1828, his own last year. For the volcanic, wildly imaginative Frenchman Hector Berlioz (1803–69), Beethoven was little short of a deity, the incarnation of the spirit of revolution. But his contemporary Felix Mendelssohn (1809–47) saw, as few others did at that time, that Beethoven was also deeply rooted in the past; that he faced both forwards and backwards. His own Beethoven-inspired works could hardly be less like those of Berlioz.

Two later composers, Johannes Brahms (1833–97) and Anton Bruckner (1824–96), also found the influence of Beethoven close to overwhelming. Brahms waited until he was well in his forties before completing a first symphony: 'You've no idea how difficult it can be', he admitted, 'when such a giant marches behind you.' Bruckner was obsessed with the *Ninth Symphony*, as was his pupil Gustav Mahler (1860–1911), composer of two choral symphonies, one of which – the '*Resurrection*' – strongly echoes Beethoven's *Ninth*.

For the spectacularly self-assured Richard Wagner (1813–83) Beethoven was not so much a perfect genius as a great prophet – of Wagner himself, that is. He saw the orchestral-vocal progression of the *Ninth Symphony* as symbolic of music's struggle to get back from half-articulate instrumental language to vocal-orchestral-dramatic wholeness – what he was to call 'The total work of art'. Wagner also spearheaded a campaign against Mendelssohn's style of conducting Beethoven, which had favoured rhythmic precision and dance energy. What Wagner achieved was a romantic opening-out of Beethoven performance, a freeing of tempo and an underlining of the music's long melodic sweep. In some ways the Mendelssohn–Wagner conflict in performing Beethoven's works continues today, some musicians favouring the rhythmic 'classical' approach, others the lyrical 'romantic'.

Beethoven has continued to stimulate or provoke composers up to the present day. In his *Fourth Quartet*, Sir Michael Tippett (1905–) builds a whole movement around an idea from the *Große Fuge*, while in his very last work, the *Viola Sonata*, Dmitri Shostakovich (1906–75) dwells extensively on the famous theme from the '*Moonlight*' *Piano Sonata*.

For many years Beethoven was the official 'greatest composer'. The years since World War Two have seen the rise of another contender, Wolfgang Amadeus Mozart (1756–91). The bicentenary of Mozart's death in 1991 was celebrated with something of the religious fervour of the Viennese Beethoven exhibition of 1902. Perhaps people are less drawn now to the idea of Beethovenian 'struggle' than to that of Mozartian 'effortless inspiration', although even Mozart could sometimes find that effort was needed in reaching the final, perfect form of a work.

But it is worth remembering that Beethoven is the only one of those that are today held to be the supreme great composers to have been consistently considered great by every generation since his death. And his musical message has shown an extraordinary ability to adapt to the needs of each age. In the early 1980s, for instance, it was often claimed that the symphonies had become *too* popular, that they had been played to death. But then came the 'period instrument' movement, which attempted to restore instruments and performing styles of Beethoven's own time. Suddenly the music ceased to be familiar, and all manner of new questions arose. It was discovered, for instance, that many published editions of Beethoven had been 'improved' by nineteenth-century musicians. When Beethoven's original ideas were restored, they often turned out to be more interesting, and sometimes more radical, than anyone had suspected.

At the same time, popular feeling about Beethoven has also shown signs of change. The use of the 'joy' theme from the *Ninth Symphony* as the European Economic Community's anthem might have looked like the kiss of death for what was once a bold new idea. But then came the revolutions in Eastern Europe, with performances of *Fidelio* and the *Ninth Symphony* becoming focal points of popular rejection of the old, repressive Communist order. When the Berlin Wall came down at last, the climax of the celebrations was another performance of the *Ninth*, with Schiller's original *Freiheit* ('Freedom') substituted for the familiar *Freude* ('Joy').

How is it that the music is able to go on renewing itself from age to age? The pianist Artur Schnabel once remarked that Beethoven's greatest works were 'greater than they can be played' – that no performance, however sympathetic, could embrace everything. Perhaps this also true in a broader sense: the music's character and originality are so multi-faceted that there is always more than can be comprehended at any one time.

The composer Igor Stravinsky (1882–1971) called the *Große Fuge* 'that absolutely contemporary work that will be contemporary for ever'. He could have said the same of many other Beethoven pieces. For all his emotive, over-wrought language, Franz Grillparzer could have been right: Beethoven's music may well 'live for all time'.

LUDWIG VAN BEETHOVEN: RECOMMENDED READING

GENERAL TITLES (introductory)

Denis Matthews: *Beethoven* [The Master Musicians Series]
   (Dent, London, 1985)

GENERAL TITLES (more specialist)

Barry Cooper (ed.): *The Beethoven Companion* (Thames &
   Hudson, London 1991)

PERSONAL RECOLLECTIONS

Franz Wegeler & Ferdinand Ries: *Remembering Beethoven* (André
   Deutsch, London, 1988)
Gerhard von Breuning: *Memories of Beethoven* (Cambridge
   University Press, Cambridge, 1992)

CORRESPONDENCE

The Letters of Beethoven (3 vols.), collected, translated and
   edited by Emily Anderson (Macmillan, London 1961)

MUSIC (commentary and analysis)

Robert Simpson: *Beethoven Symphonies* (BBC Music Guides,
   London 1970)
Basil Lam: *Beethoven String Quartets* (BBC Music Guides,
   London 1975)
Donald Francis Tovey: *Beethoven* (Oxford University Press,
   London 1944)
Denis Arnold & Nigel Fortune (ed.): *The Beethoven Companion*
   (Faber & Faber, London 1971)

LUDWIG VAN BEETHOVEN: COMPLETE LIST OF WORKS

Most of Beethoven's works are catalogued according to Opus (work) numbers and these are roughly based on the date of composition.

Those works that have no opus numbers are prefaced by WoO (*Werk ohne Opuszahl* = work without opus number). In addition, Hess numbers were assigned to further works in 1957.

Dates are given where known.

Op.1	*Piano Trios Nos.1–3*, E major, G major, C minor (1795)
Op.2	*Piano Sonatas Nos.1–3*, F minor, A major, C major (1795)
Op.3	*String Trio*, E flat major (by 1794)
Op.4	*String Quintet* (arr. of Op.103), E flat major (1795)
Op.5	*Cello Sonatas Nos.1–2*, F major, G minor (1796)
Op.6	*Piano Sonata for 4 hands*, D major (1797)
Op.7	*Piano Sonata No.4*, E flat major (1797)
Op.8	*String Trio, 'Serenade'*, D major (1797)
Op.9	*String Trios Nos.1–3*, G major, D major, C minor (1798)
Op.10	*Piano Sonatas Nos.5–7*, C minor, F major, D major (1795–98)
Op.11	*Trio (piano, clarinet or violin, cello)*, B flat major (1797)
Op.12	*Violin Sonatas Nos.1–3*, D major, A major, E flat major (1798)
Op.13	*Piano Sonata No.8, 'Pathétique'*, C minor (1798)
Op.14	*Piano Sonatas Nos.9–10*, E major, G minor (1798–99)
Op.15	*Piano Concerto No.1*, C major (1795)
Op.16	*Piano Quintet*, E flat major (1796)
Op.17	*Horn Sonata*, F major (1800)

Op.18	*String Quartets Nos.1–6*, F major, G major, D major, C minor, A major, B flat major (1800)
Op.19	*Piano Concerto No.2*, B flat major (1798)
Op.20	*Septet*, E flat major (1800)
Op.21	*Symphony No.1*, C major (1800)
Op.22	*Piano Sonata No.11*, B flat major (1800)
Op.23	*Violin Sonata*, A minor (1800)
Op.24	*Violin Sonata*, '*Spring*', F major (1801)
Op.25	*Serenade for flute, violin, viola*, D major (1801)
Op.26	*Piano Sonata No.12*, A flat major (1801)
Op.27	*Piano Sonatas Nos.13–14* ('*quasi una fantasia*'), E flat major, '*Moonlight*' C sharp (1801)
Op.28	*Piano Sonata No.15*, '*Pastorale*', D major(1801)
Op.29	*String Quintet*, C major (1801)
Op.30	*Violin Sonatas Nos.1–3*, A major, C minor, G major (1802)
Op.31	*Piano Sonatas Nos.16–18*, G major, D minor, E flat major (1802)
Op.32	*Song* '*An die Hoffnung*' (1805)
Op.33	*7 'Bagatelles'* for piano (1802)
Op.34	*6 Variations* on original theme for piano, F major (1802)
Op.35	*15 Variations and fugue* on theme from '*Prometheus*', *Eroica Variations*, E flat major (1802)
Op.36	*Symphony No.2*, D major (1802)
Op.37	*Piano Concerto No.3*, C minor (c.1800)
Op.38	*Piano Trio* (arr. of Op.20), E flat major (1802-3)
Op.39	*Twelve Preludes* through all twelve major keys (1789)
Op.40	*Violin Romance*, G major (1798–1802)
Op.41	*Serenade* (arr. of Op.25), D major (1803)
Op.42	*Notturno* (arr. of Op.8), D major (1803)
Op.43	*Overture and Ballet*, '*Die Geschöpfe des Prometheus*' (1801)
Op.44	*Piano Trio, 14 Variations*, E flat major (1802–3)
Op.45	*Three marches for 4 hands*, C major, E flat major, D major (1803)
Op.46	*Song 'Adelaide'* (1795)
Op.47	*Violin Sonata*, '*Kreutzer*', A major (1803)
Op.48	*6 Gellert songs* (1802)
Op.49	*Piano Sonatas Nos.19–20*, G minor, G major (1802)

Op.50	*Violin Romance*, F major (1798–1802)
Op.51	*Rondos* for piano, C major, G major (1796–98)
Op.52	*8 songs* (1790–96)
Op.53	*Piano Sonata No.21, 'Waldstein'*, C major (1804)
Op.54	*Piano Sonata No.22*, F major (1804)
Op.55	*Symphony No.3, 'Eroica'*, E flat major (1803)
Op.56	*Triple Concerto* for piano, violin, cello, C major (1804)
Op.57	*Piano Sonata No.23, 'Appassionata'*, F minor (1805)
Op.58	*Piano Concerto No.4*, G major (1806)
Op.59	*String Quartets Nos.1–3, 'Razumovsky'*, F major, E minor, C major (1806)
Op.60	*Symphony No.4*, B flat major (1806)
Op.61	*Violin Concerto*, D major (1806)
Op.62	*Overture – Coriolan* (1807)
Op.64	*Op.3* transcribed for cello and piano, E flat major
Op.65	*Scena* and Aria *'Ah Perfido!'* (1796)
Op.66	*Variation* for piano and cello on *'Ein Mädchen oder Weibchen'* from *Die Zauberflöte*, F major (1796)
Op.67	*Symphony No.5*, C minor (1808)
Op.68	*Symphony No.6, 'Pastoral '*, F major (1808)
Op.69	*Cello Sonata*, A major (1808)
Op.70	*Piano Trios Nos.1–2*, D major, E flat major (1808)
Op.71	*Sextet*, B flat major (1796)
Op.72	*Fidelio* (1805, rev. 1806, 1814)
Op.73	*Piano Concerto No.5, 'Emperor'*, E flat major (1809)
Op.74	*String Quartet, 'Harp'*, E flat major (1809)
Op.75	*6 Songs* (1809)
Op.76	*6 Variations* for piano, D major (1810)
Op.77	*Fantaisie*, G minor / B flat major (1810)
Op.78	*Piano Sonata No.24*, F sharp major (1809)
Op.79	*Piano Sonata No.25, 'Sonatina'*, G minor (1809)
Op.80	*Choral Fantasia* (1808)
Op.81a	*Piano Sonata No.26, 'Les Adieux'*, E flat major (1810)
Op.81b	*Sextet*, E flat major (c.1795)
Op.82	*4 ariettas and duet* (c.1809)
Op.83	*3 Goethe songs* (1810)
Op.84	*Incidental music, 'Egmont'* (1810)
Op.85	*Oratorio, Christus am Ölberge* (1803)
Op.86	*Mass*, C major (1807)

Op.87	*Trio*, C major (1795)
Op.88	Song, '*Das Glück der Freundschaft*' (1803)
Op.89	*Polonaise* for piano, C major (1814)
Op.90	*Piano Sonata No.27*, E minor (1814)
Op.91	'*Battle Symphony*' (1813)
Op.92	*Symphony No.7*, A major (1812)
Op.93	*Symphony No.8*, F major (1812)
Op.94	Song, '*An die Hoffnung*' (?1815)
Op.95	*String Quartet*, F minor (1810)
Op.96	*Violin Sonata*, G major (1812)
Op.97	*Piano Trio*, '*Archduke*', B flat major (1811)
Op.98	*An die ferne Geliebte*, song cycle (1816)
Op.99	Song, '*Der Mann von Wort*' (1816)
Op.100	Song, '*Merkenstein*' (1814)
Op.101	*Piano Sonata No.28*, A major (1816)
Op.102	*Cello Sonatas Nos.1–2*, C major, D major (1815)
Op.103	*Octet for wind instruments*, E flat major (1792–93)
Op.104	*String Quintet* (arr. of Op.1), C minor (1817)
Op.105	*Six National Airs with variations* (c.1818)
Op.106	*Piano Sonata No.29*, '*Hammerklavier*', B flat major (1818)
Op.107	*Ten National Airs with variations* (c.1818)
Op.108	*25 Scottish songs* (1815–16)
Op.109	*Piano Sonata No.30*, E major (1820)
Op.110	*Piano Sonata No.31*, A flat major (1822)
Op.111	*Piano Sonata No.32*, C minor (1822)
Op.112	'*Meersstille und Glückliche Fahrt*' ('Calm Sea and Prosperous Voyage') (1815)
Op.113	*Incidental music*, '*Die Ruinen von Athen*' (1811)
Op.115	*Overture*, '*Namensfeier*', C major (1815)
Op.116	*Tremate, empi, tremate* (1801–2)
Op.117	*Incidental music*, '*König Stephan*' (1811)
Op.118	*Elegischer Gesang* '*Sanft wie du lebtest*' (1814)
Op.119	*11 Bagatelles* for piano (1822)
Op.120	*33 Variations on a waltz by Diabelli* (1819–23)
Op.121a	*Piano Trio*, '*Kakadu*', C major (1803)
Op.121b	*Opferlied* (1823–24)
Op.122	*Bundeslied* '*In allen guten Stunden*' (1823–24)
Op.123	'*Missa solemnis*', D major (1823)
Op.124	*Overture*, '*Die Weihe des Hauses*' (1822)

Op.125	*Symphony No.9, 'Choral'*, D minor (1824)
Op.126	*6 Bagatelles* for piano (1823)
Op.127	*String Quartet No.12*, E flat major (1825)
Op.128	Song, *'Der Kuss'* (?1822)
Op.129	*'Rondo a capriccio'*, G major (1825–26)
Op.130	*String Quartet No.13*, B flat major (1826)
Op.131	*String Quartet No.14*, C sharp minor (1826)
Op.132	*String Quartet No.15*, A minor (1825)
Op.133	*Große Fuge*, B flat major (1826)
Op.134	*Op.133* arr. for piano duet (1826)
Op.135	*String Quartet No.16*, F major (1826)
Op.136	*Cantata, 'Der Glorreiche Augenblick'* (The Glorious Moment) (1814)
Op.137	*Fugue*, D major (1817)
Op.138	*Leonora No.1* (1805), (*Leonora No.2* Op.72a 1805, *Leonora No.3* Op.72b 1806)
WoO 1	*Ballet, 'Ritterballett'* (1790–91)
WoO 2a	*Triumphal March* for *Tarpeja*, C major (1813)
WoO 2b	Introduction to Act 2 for *Tarpeja* (1813)
WoO 3	*Gratulations-Menuet*, E flat major (1822)
WoO 4	*Piano Concerto*, E flat major (1784)
WoO 5	*Violin Concerto*, C major (frag.) (c.1790–92)
WoO 6	*Rondo*, B flat major (before 1794)
WoO 7	*Twelve minuets* (1795)
WoO 8	*Twelve German dances* (1795)
WoO 9	*Six minuets*
WoO 10	*Six minuets* (?1795)
WoO 11	*Seven Ländler* (?1798)
WoO 13	*Twelve German dances*
WoO 14	*Twelve contredanses* (1802)
WoO 15	*Six Ländler* (1801–2)
WoO 18	*March 'für die böhmische Landwehr'*, F major (1809)
WoO 19	*March*, F major (1810)
WoO 20	*March with Trio*, C major (before 1823)
WoO 21	*Polonaise*, D major (1810)
WoO 22	*Ecossaise*, D major (1810)
WoO 23	*Ecossaise*, G major (?1810)
WoO 24	*March*, D major (1816)
WoO 25	*Rondino*, E flat major (1793)
WoO 26	*Allegro and Minuet* for 2 flutes, G major (1792)

WoO 28	*Variations on 'Là ci darem la mano' from Mozart's Don Giovanni*, C major (?1795)
WoO 29	*March*, B flat major (1798)
WoO 30	*Three Equali*, B flat major (1812)
WoO 33/1	*Adagio* for mechanical clock, F major (?c.1799)
WoO 33/2	*Scherzo* for mechanical clock, G major (1799–1800)
WoO 33/3	*Allegro* for mechanical clock, G major (?c.1799)
WoO 33/4	*Allegro*, for mechanical clock?, C major (?c.1794)
WoO 33/5	*Minuet*, for mechanical clock?, C major (?c.1794)
WoO 32	*Duet* for viola and cello, E flat major (1796–97)
WoO 34	*Duet* for 2 violins, A major (1822)
WoO 35	*Canon* (1825)
WoO 36	*Three Quartets*, E flat major, D major, C major (1785)
WoO 37	*Trio*, G major (1786)
WoO 38	*Piano Trio*, E flat major (?1791)
WoO 39	*Allegretto*, B flat major (1812)
WoO 40	*Variations on 'Se vuol ballare'* from *Le nozze di Figaro* for piano and violin, F major (1792–93)
WoO 41	*Rondo* for piano and violin, G major (1793–94)
WoO 42	*Six German dances* for piano and violin (1796)
WoO 43a	*Sonatina* for piano and mandolin, C minor (1796)
WoO 43b	*Adagio* for piano and mandolin, E flat major (1796)
WoO 44a	*Sonatina* for piano for mandolin, C major (1796)
WoO 44b	*Andante and Variations* for piano and mandolin, D major (1796)
WoO 45	*Variations* for piano and cello *on 'See the conqu'ring hero comes'* from *Judas Maccabaeus*, G major (1796)
WoO 46	*Variations* for piano and cello *on 'Bei Männern, welche Liebe fühlen'* from *Die Zauberflöte*, E flat major (1801)
WoO 47	*Three Piano Sonatas*, E flat major, F minor, D major (?1783)
WoO 48	*Rondo* for piano, C major (1783)
WoO 49	*Rondo* for piano, A major (?1783)
WoO 50	*Piano Sonata*, F major (before 1793)
WoO 51	*Piano Sonata*, C major (frag.) (?1797–98)
WoO 52	*Presto* for piano, C minor (?1795)
WoO 53	*Allegretto* for piano, C minor (1796–97)
WoO 54	*Bagatelle 'Lustig-Traurig'* for piano, C major (?1802)
WoO 55	*Prelude* for piano, F minor (before 1805)

WoO 56   *Allegretto* for piano, C major (1803)

WoO 57   *Andante* for piano ('*Andante favori*'), F major (1803)

WoO 58   *Cadenzas* to first movement and finale of Mozart's *Piano Concerto*, D minor, K466

WoO 59   *Bagatelle* for piano '*Für Elise*', A minor (1808, 1810)

WoO 60   *Bagatelle* for piano, B flat major (1818)

WoO 61   *Allegretto* for piano, B minor (1821)

WoO 61a   *Allegretto Quasi Andante* for piano, G minor (1825)

WoO 63   *Nine Variations* for piano *on a march by Dressler*, C minor (1782)

WoO 64   *Six Variations* for harp and piano *on a Swiss song*, F major (before 1793)

WoO 65   *Twenty-four Variations* for piano *on Righini's arietta* '*Venni amore*', D major (1790–91)

WoO 66   *Thirteen variations* for piano *on* '*Es war einmal ein alter Mann*' from Dittersdorf's *Das rote Käppchen*, A major (1792)

WoO 67   *Eight variations* for piano *on a theme by Count Waldstein*, C major (?1792)

WoO 68   *Twelve variations* for piano *on the* '*Menuet à la Vigano*' *from Haibel's Le nozze disturbate*, C major (1795)

WoO 69   *Nine variations* for piano *on* '*Quant' è più bello*' *from Paisiello's La molinara*, A major (1795)

WoO 70   *Six variations* for piano *on* '*Nel cor più non mi sento*' *from La molinara*, G major (1795)

WoO 71   *Twelve variations* for piano *on a Russian dance from Wranitsky's Das Waldmädchen*, A major (1796–97)

WoO 72   *Eight variations* for piano *on* '*Une fièvre brûlante*' *from Grétry's Richard Coeur de Lion*, C major (?1795)

WoO 73   *Ten variations* for piano *on* '*La stressa, le stressissima*' *from Salieri's Falstaff*, B flat major (1799)

WoO 74   *Six variations* for piano *on* '*Ich denke dein*', D major (1799, 1803)

WoO 75   *Seven variations* for piano *on* '*Kind, willst du ruhig schlafen*' *from Winter's Das unterbrochene Opferfest*, F major (1799)

WoO 76   *Six variations* for piano *on* '*Tändeln und Scherzen*' *from Süssmayr's Soliman II*, F major (1799)

WoO 77   *Six variations* for piano *on an original theme*, G major (1800)

WoO 78	*Seven variations* for piano *on 'God Save the King'*, C major (1802/3)
WoO 79	*Five variations* for piano *on 'Rule Britannia'*, D major (1803)
WoO 80	*Thirty-two variations* for piano *on an original theme*, C minor (1806)
WoO 81	*Allemande* for piano, A major (1793)
WoO 82	*Minuet* for piano, E flat major (before 1805)
WoO 84	*Waltz* for piano, E flat major (1824)
WoO 85	*Waltz* for piano, D major (1825)
WoO 86	*Ecossaise*, E flat major (1825)
WoO 87	*Cantata on the death of Emperor Joseph II* (1790–91)
WoO 88	*Cantata on the accession of Emperor Leopold II* (1790)
WoO 89	Aria, *'Prüfung des Kussens' 'Meine weise Mutter spricht'* (c.1790–92)
WoO 90	Aria, *'Mit Mädeln sich vertragen '*(c.1790–92)
WoO 91	*Two arias for Umlauf's Singspiel Die Schöne Schusterin (?1795–96)*
WoO 92	*Scena and aria, 'Primo amore'* (c.1790–92)
WoO 92a	*Scena and aria, 'No, non turbati'* (1801–2)
WoO 93	*Duet from Olimpiade, 'Ne' giorni tuoi felici'* (1802–3)
WoO 94	*Germania, finale of Die gute Nachricht* (1814)
WoO 95	Choral work, *'Ihr weisen Gründer'* (1814)
WoO 96	*Incidental music, Leonore Prohaska* (1815)
WoO 97	*Es ist vollbracht, finale of Die Ehrenpforten* (1815)
WoO 98	*'Wo Sich die Pulse', chorus for Die Weihe des Hauses (1822)*
WoO 100	*Schuppanzigh ist ein Lump* (1801)
WoO 101	*Graf, Graf, Graf, Graf* (1802)
WoO 102	*Abschiedsgesang 'Die Stunde schlägt'* (1814)
WoO 103	*Cantata Campestre 'Un lieto brindisi'* (1814)
WoO 104	*Gesang der Mönche 'Rasch tritt der Tod'* (1817)
WoO 105	*Hochzeitslied 'Auf Freunde, singt dem Gott der Ehen'* (1817)
WoO 106	*Birthday Cantata for Prince Lobkowitz* (1823)
WoO 107	Song, *'Schilderung eines Mädchens'* (?1783)
WoO 108	Song, *'An einen Säugling'* (?1784)
WoO 109	Song, *'Trinklied'* (?1790)
WoO 110	Song, *'Elegie auf den Tod eines* (?before 1793)
WoO 111	Song, *'Punchslied'* (c.1790–92)

WoO 112	Song, '*An Laura*' (?1792)
WoO 113	Song, '*Klage*' (?1790)
WoO 114	Song, '*Selbstgespräch*' (?1792)
WoO 115	Song, '*An Minna*' (?1792)
WoO 116	Song, '*Que le temps me dure*' (1793)
WoO 117	Song, '*Der freie Mann*' (1792, rev. 1794) {qsp?
WoO 118	Two songs:
	♦ '*Seufzer eines Ungeliebten*'
	♦ '*Gegenliebe*' (1794–95)
WoO 119	Song, '*O care selve*' (1794)
WoO 120	Song, '*Man strebt die Flamme zu verhehlen*' (c.1800–2)
WoO 121	*Abschiedsgesang an Wiens Bürger* (1796)
WoO 122	*Kriegslied der Österreicher* (1797)
WoO 123	Song, '*Zärtliche Liebe*' (?1795)
WoO 124	Song, '*La partenza*' (?1795–96)
WoO 125	Song, '*La tiranna*' (1798–99)
WoO 126	*Opferlied* (1794, rev. 1801–2)
WoO 127	Song, '*Neue Liebe, neues Leben*' (1798/9)
WoO 128	Song, '*Plaisir d'aimer*' (1798–99)
WoO 129	Song, '*Der Wachtelschlag*' (1803)
WoO 130	Song, '*Gedenke mein*' (?1804–5, rev. 1819–20)
WoO 132	Song, '*Als die Geliebte sich trennen wollte*' (1806)
WoO 133	Song, '*In questa tomba oscura*' (1807)
WoO 134	Song, '*Sehnsucht*' (1807–8)
WoO 135	Song, '*Die laute Klage*' (?c.1815)
WoO 136	Song, '*Andenken*' (1809)
WoO 137	Song, '*Lied aus der Ferne*' (1809)
WoO 138	Song, '*Der Jüngling in der Fremde*' (1809)
WoO 139	Song, '*Der Liebende*' (1809)
WoO 140	Song, '*An die Geliebte*', 2 versions (1811; ?1814)
WoO 141	Song, '*Der Gesang der Nachtigal*' (1813)
WoO 142	Song, '*Der Bardengeist*' (1813)
WoO 143	Song, '*Des Kriegers*' (1814)
WoO 144	Song, '*Merkenstein*' (1814)
WoO 145	Song, '*Das Geheimnis*' (1815)
WoO 146	Song, '*Sehnsucht*' (1815–16)
WoO 147	Song, '*Ruf vom Berge*' (1816)
WoO 148	Song, '*So oder so*' (1817)
WoO 149	Song, '*Resignation*' (1817)
WoO 150	*Abendlied unterm gestirnten Himmel* (1820)

WoO 151	Song, *'Der edle Mensch sei hülfreich und gut'* (1823)
WoO 152	25 Irish folksongs
WoO 153	20 Irish folksongs
WoO 154	12 Irish folksongs
WoO 155	26 Welsh folksongs
WoO 156	12 Scottish folksongs
WoO 157	12 folksongs of various nationality
WoO 158a	23 folksongs of various nationality
WoO 158b	7 British folksongs
WoO 158c	6 folksongs of various nationality
WoO 159	Contrapuntal study, *Im Arm der Liebe* (?1795)
WoO 160/1	Contrapuntal study, *?O care selve* (?1795)
WoO 160/2	Canon (?1795)
WoO 161	Canon, *Ewig dein*
WoO 163	Canon, *Kurz ist der Schmerz* (1813)
WoO 164	Canon, *Freundschaft ist die Quelle* (1814)
WoO 165	Canon, *Glück zum neuen Jahr* (1815)
WoO 166	Canon, *Kurz ist der Schmerz* (1815)
WoO 167	Canon, *Brauchle, Linke*
WoO 168/1	Puzzle Canon, *Lerne schweigen* (1815–16)
WoO 168/2	Canon, *Rede, rede* (1815–16)
WoO 169	Puzzle Canon, *Ich küsse Sie* (1816)
WoO 170	Canon, *Ars longa, vita brevis* (1816)
WoO 171	Canon, *Glück fehl' dir vor allem* (1817)
WoO 172	Canon, *Ich bitt' dich, schreib' mir die Es-Scala auf*
WoO 173	Puzzle Canon, *Hol' euch der Teufel!* (1819)
WoO 174	*Glaube und hoffe* (1819)
WoO 175	Puzzle canons, *Sankt Petrus war ein Fels; Bernardus war ein Sankt* (1819–20)
WoO 176	Canon, *Glück zum neuen Jahr!* (1819)
WoO 177	Canon, *Bester Magistrat, Ihr friert*
WoO 178	Canon, *Signor Abate*
WoO 179	Canon, *Alles Gute! alles Schöne* (1819)
WoO 180	Canon, *Hoffmann, sei ja kein Hofmann* (1820)
WoO 181/1	Canon, *Gedenket heute an Baden* (?1820)
WoO 181/2	Canon, *Gehabt euch wohl* (?1820)
WoO 181/3	Canon, *Tugent ist kein leerer Name* (?1820)
WoO 182	Canon, *O Tobias!* (1821)
WoO 183	Canon, *Bester Herr Graf, Sie sind ein Schaf!* (1823)
WoO 184	Canon, *Falstafferel, lass' dich sehen!* (1823)

WoO 185	Canon, *Edel sei der Mensch* (1823)
WoO 186	Canon, *Te solo adoro* (1824)
WoO 187	Canon, *Schwenke dich ohne Schwänke!* (1824)
WoO 188	Puzzle Canon, *Gott ist eine feste Burg* (1825)
WoO 189	Canon, *Doktor, sperrt das Tor dem Tod* (1825)
WoO 190	Puzzle Canon, *Ich war Hier, Doktor* (1825)
WoO 191	Canon, *Kühl, nicht lau* (1825)
WoO 192	Puzzle Canon, *Ars longa, vita brevis* (1825)
WoO 193	Puzzle Canon, *Ars longa, vita brevis*
WoO 194	Puzzle Canon, *Si non per portas, per muros* (1825)
WoO 195	Canon, *Freu' dich des Lebens* (1825)
WoO 196	Canon, *Es muss sein* (1826)
WoO 197	Canon, *Da ist das Werk* (1826)
WoO 198	Puzzle Canon, *Wir irren allesamt* (1826)
WoO 203	Puzzle Canon, *Das Schöne zu dem Guten* (1825)
WoO 204	Canon, *Holz, Holz, geigt die Quartette so* (1825)
Hess 12	*Oboe Concerto*, F major (lost) (?c.1792–93)
Hess 13	*Romance* (frag.) (1786)
Hess 19	*Quintet*, E flat major (?1793)
Hess 28	*Trio for the Minuet of Op.9 No.1*, G major (1797–98)
Hess 33	*Minuet for String Quintet*, A flat major (c.1790)
Hess 34	Arr. of Op.14 *No.1 for String Quartet*, F major (1801–2)
Hess 40	*Prelude for String Quintet*, D minor (?1817)
Hess 41	*String Quintet*, C major (frag.) (1826)
Hess 46	*Violin Sonata*, A major (frag.) (c.1790–92)
Hess 48	*Allegretto*, E flat major (c.1790–92)
Hess 64	*Fugue* for piano, C major (1795)
Hess 65	'*Concert Finale*' for piano, C major (1820–1)
Hess 69	*Allegretto* for piano in C minor (1796/7)
Hess 107	*Grenadiermarsch* for mechanical clock, F major (?c.1798)
Hess 115	Opera, *Vestas Feuer* (frag.) (1803)
Hess 129	Song, '*Que le temps me dure*' (WoO 116, first version)
Hess 130	Song, '*Que le temps me dure*' (WoO 116, second version)
Hess 133	Folksong, '*Das liebe Kätzchen*'
Hess 134	Folksong, '*Der Knabe auf dem Berge*'
Hess 151	Song, '*Traute Henriette*' (c.1790–92)

Hess 168	Folksong, '*Air français*'
Hess 229	Canon, *Languisco e moro* (1803)
Hess 263	Canon, *Te solo adoro* (?1824)
Hess 264	Canon, *Te solo adoro* (?1824)
Hess 274	Canon (1803)
Hess 275	Canon (1803)
Hess 276	Canon, *Herr Graf, ich komme zu fragen* (?1797)
Hess 277	Canon, *Esel aller Esel* (1826)
Hess 300	Canon, *Liebe mich, werter Weissenbach* (1819–20)

◆ *Contrapuntal exercises prepared for Haydn and Albrechtsberger* (Hess 29–31, 233–246)

◆ *Exercises in Italian declamation prepared for Salieri* (WoO 99; Hess 208–232)

LUDWIG VAN BEETHOVEN: RECOMMENDED RECORDINGS

The following list of recommended recordings is included as a guide to some of the interpretations of Beethoven's work available at the time of writing. It is by no means intended as an exhaustive catalogue.

The works are listed first, followed by details of the recordings, the artists, record label and disc number. All numbers apply to the compact disc format, but many recordings can be bought on conventional tape cassette.

OPERA

Opus 72   **Fidelio**
♦   Ludwig (Leonore), Vickers (Florestan), Berry (Don Pizarro), Frick (Rocco), Hallstein (Marzelline), Unger, (Jacquino), Cras (Don Fernando), Wehofschitz (First Prisoner), Wolansky (Second Prisoner), Philharmonia Ch. and Orch., Klemperer
   ⊗ EMI CMS7 69324-2

CHORAL AND SOLO VOCAL

Opus 86   **Mass in C major**
Opus 112   **Meersstille und glückliche Fahrt**
Opus 65   **Ah! Perfido**
♦   Margiono (soprano), Robbin (mezzo), Kendall (tenor), Miles (bass), Monteverdi Ch. and English Baroque Soloists, Gardiner
   ⊗ Archiv 435 391-2 (with period instruments)

Opus 123   **Mass in D major, 'Missa Solemnis'**
♦   Tomowa-Sintow (soprano), Baltsa (contralto), Krenn (tenor), van Dam (bass), Vienna Singverein & Berlin Philh. Orch., von Karajan (two CDs)
   ⊗ DG 423 913-2 (c/w Mozart's *The Coronation Mass*)

Opus 85   **Christ on the Mount of Olives**
♦   Pick-Hieronimi (soprano), Anderson (tenor), von Halem
   (bass), Lyon National Ch. & Orch., Baudo
      ⊗ HM HMC 90 5181

Opus 117   **King Stephen, incidental music**
Opus 118   **Elegischer Gesang**
Opus 121b   **Opferlied**
Opus 122   **Bundeslied**
Opus 112   **Meersstille und glückliche Fahrt**
♦   Haywood (soprano), Ambrosian Singers & LSO, Tilson
   Thomas
      ⊗ CBS CD 76404

Opus 98   **An die ferne Geliebte**
Opus 46   **Adelaide**
WoO 123   **Zärtliche liebe**
Opus 82   **L'Amante Impaziente, Nos.3–4**
WoO 133   **In Questa Tomba Obscura**
Opus 52   **Maigesang, No.4**
Opus 75   **Es war einmal ein König**
♦   Fischer-Dieskau (baritone), Demus (pf)
      ⊗ DG 415 189-2 (c/w Brahms' *Lieder*)

Opus 80   **Fantasia for Piano, Chorus and Orchestra in
         C minor** *see* CONCERTOS

SYMPHONIES

Opus 21   **Symphony No.1 in C major**
Opus 36   **Symphony No.2 in D major**
Opus 55   **Symphony No.3 in E flat major**
Opus 60   **Symphony No.4 in B flat major**
Opus 67   **Symphony No.5 in C minor**
Opus 68   **Symphony No.6 in F major 'Pastoral'**
Opus 92   **Symphony No.7 in A major**
Opus 93   **Symphony No.8 in F major**
Opus 125   **Symphony No.9 in D minor 'Choral'**
♦   COE, Harnoncourt
      ⊗ Teldec 2292 46452-2 (5) (brilliant, innovative, but not to all tastes)

Symphonies 1–9
♦ North German Radio Symphony Orch., Wand
    ⊗ BMG / RCA RD 60090 (an excellent, less controversial alternative)

Opus 21   **Symphony No.1 in C major**
Opus 67   **Symphony No.5 in C minor**
♦ Leipzig Gewandhaus Orch., Masur
    ⊗ Philips 426 782-2

Opus 36   **Symphony No.2 in D major**
Opus 60   **Symphony No.4 in B flat major**
♦ North German Radio Symphony Orch., Wand
    ⊗ BMG / RCA RD 60058

Opus 55   **Symphony No.3 in E flat major, 'Eroica'**
Opus 84   **Egmont Overture**
♦ Dresden Staatskapelle, Davis
    ⊗ Philips 434120-2

Opus 67   **Symphony No.5 in C minor**
Opus 92   **Symphony No.7 in A major**
♦ Vienna Philh. Orch., Kleiber
    ⊗ DG 447 400 2

Opus 68   **Symphony No.6 in F major, 'Pastoral'**
Opus 67   **Symphony No.5 in C minor**
♦ North German Radio Symphony Orch., Wand
    ⊗ BMG / RCA 09026-2

Opus 92   **Symphony No.7 in A major**
Opus 93   **Symphony No.8 in F major**
♦ LSO, Morris
    ⊗ Pickwick PCD 918

Opus 125 **Symphony No.9 in D minor, 'Choral'**
♦ Rogers (soprano), Jones (mezzo), Bronder (tenor), Terfel
   (bass), Royal Liverpool Philh. Ch. & Orch., Mackerras
    ⊗ EMI Eminence CD-EMX 2186

OTHER ORCHESTRAL WORKS

Opus 113 **Overture: The Ruins of Athens**
Opus 62   **Overture: Coriolan**
Opus 138 **Overture: Leonore No.1**
Opus 72a **Overture: Leonore No.3**
Opus 43   **Overture: The Creatures of Prometheus**
Opus 84   **Overture: Egmont**
Opus 117 **Overture: King Stephen**
♦   Berlin Philharmonic Orch., von Karajan
   ⊗ DG 427 256 2

Opus 113 **Overture: The Ruins of Athens, incidental music, excerpts**
♦   Beecham Choral Society & Royal Philh., Orch., Beecham
   ⊗ EMI CDM7 64385-2

Opus 117 **King Stephen, incidental music** *see* CHORAL AND SOLO VOCAL

CONCERTOS

Opus 15   **Piano Concerto No.1 in C major**
Opus 19   **Piano Concerto No.2 in B flat major**
Opus 37   **Piano Concerto No.3 in C minor**
Opus 58   **Piano Concerto No.4 in G major**
Opus 73   **Piano Concerto No.5 in E flat major**
Opus 56* **Triple Concerto in C major**
♦   Fleisher (pf), Cleveland Orch., Szell, Istomin* (pf),
        Stern (vn), Rose (vc), Philadelphia Orch., Ormandy
   ⊗ Sony Classical CD 46549

Opus 15   **Piano Concerto No.1 in C major**
Opus 19   **Piano Concerto No.2 in B flat major**
♦   Kempff (pf), Berlin Philh., Orch., Leitner
   ⊗ DG 419 856-2

Opus 37   **Piano Concerto No.3 in C minor**
Opus 58   **Piano Concerto No.4 in G major**
♦   Perahia (pf), Concertgebouw Orch., Haitink
   ⊗ CBS CD 39814

Opus 73   **Piano Concerto No.5 in E flat major**
Opus 56* **Triple Concerto in C major**
♦   Fischer (pf), Cleveland Orch., Szell, Istomin* (pf),
    Stern (vn), Rose (vc), Philadelphia Orch., Ormandy
    ⊗ Sony Classical CD 46549

Opus 80   **Fantasia in C major for Piano, Chorus and
          Orchestra**
Opus 73   **Piano Concerto No.5 in E flat major, 'Emperor'**
♦   Robert Levin (fortepiano), Orchestre Révolutionnaire
    et Romantique, Gardiner
    ⊗ Archiv 447 771 2 (with period instruments)

Opus 61   **Violin Concerto in D major**
Opus 40   **Romance for Violin and Orchestra No.1 in
          G major**
Opus 50   **Romance for Violin and Orchestra No.2 in
          F major**
♦   Gidon Kremer (vn), Chamber Orch. of Europe,
    Harnoncourt
    ⊗ Teldec 9031 74881 2

STRING QUARTETS

Opus 18   **Quartets Nos.1–6**
Opus 74   **String Quartet in E flat major, 'Harp'**
♦   Lindsay Quartet
    ⊗ ASV CD DCS 305 (3)

Opus 59   **Quartets Nos.7–9**
♦   Lindsay Quartet
    ⊗ ASV CD DCS 207 (2)

Opus 127 **Quartet No.12 in E flat major**
Opus 130 **Quartet No.13 in B flat major**
Opus 131 **Quartet No.14 in C sharp minor**
Opus 132 **Quartet No.15 in A minor**
Opus 135 **Quartet No.16 in F major**
♦   Lindsay Quartet
    ⊗ ASV CD DCS 403

Opus 59   **Quartet No.1 in F major**
Opus 130 **Quartet No.13 in B flat major**
♦   Busch Quartet
      ⊗ CBS MPK 46787 (classic mono versions recorded in 1941/42)

OTHER CHAMBER WORKS

Opus 20   **Septet in E flat major**
WoO 27   **Duet No.1 in C**
WoO 25   **Rondino in E flat major**
Opus 103 **Octet in E flat major**
WoO 29   **March in B flat**
♦   Charles Neidich (cl), Mozzafiato
      ⊗ Sony SK 53367

Opus 29   **String Quintet in C major**
♦   Academy of St Martin-in-the-Fields Chamber
      Ensemble
      ⊗ Philips 434 119-2

Opus 16   **Quintet in E flat major for Piano and Wind**
♦   Perahia (pf), members of the ECO
      ⊗ CBS CD 42099 (c/w Mozart's *Quintet for Piano and Wind*)

WoO36   **Piano Quartet in E flat major**
WoO 36   **Piano Quartet No.1 in D major**
WoO 36   **Piano Quartet No.2 in C major**
Opus 16 **Piano Quartet No.3 in E flat major**
♦   Oleg (vn), da Silva (va), Coppey (vc), Cassard (pf)
      ⊗ Audivis Valois V4715

Opus 1   **Piano Trios Nos.1–3**
Opus 70   **Piano Trio No.1 in D major, 'Ghost', No.2 in
          E flat major**
Opus 97   **Piano Trio in B flat major, 'Archduke'**
Opus 44   **14 Variations on an Original Theme**
Opus 121 **Variations on 'Ich bin der Schneider Kakadu'**
Hess 48   **Allegretto in E flat major**
♦   Beaux Arts Trio
      ⊗ Philips 438 948-2 (modern alternative including sets of variations)

Opus 1   **Piano Trio No.1 in E flat major**
Opus 97   **Piano Trio in B flat major, 'Archduke'**
♦   Trio Zingara
⊗ Collins Classics 1057-2 (modern alternative of most popular Trio)

Opus 3   **String Trio in E flat major**
♦   Polman, Zuckerman. Harrell
⊗ EMI CDS7-54198-2

Opus 9   **String Trios Nos.1–3**
♦   L'archibudelli
⊗ Sony Classical SK 48190 (played on period instruments)

Opus 25   **Serenade in D major for Flute, Violin and Viola**
WoO 37   **Trio in G major for Flute, Bassoon and Piano**
♦   Milan (fl), Azzolini (bn), and members of the Chilingirian Quartet
⊗ Chandos CHAN 9108

Opus 12   **Violin Sonatas Nos.1–3 in D major, A major and E flat major**
Opus 23   **Violin Sonata No.4 in A minor**
Opus 24   **Violin Sonata No.5 in F major, 'Spring'**
Opus 30   **Violin Sonata Nos.6–8 in A major, C minor and G major**
Opus 47   **Violin Sonata No.9 in A major, 'Kreutzer'**
Opus 96   **Violin Sonata No.10 in G major**
♦   Grumiaux (vn), Haskil (pf)
⊗ Philips 422 140-2 (3)

Opus 24   **Violin Sonata No.5 in F major, 'Spring'**
Opus 47   **Violin Sonata No.9 in A major, 'Kreutzer'**
♦   Perlman (vn), Ashkenazy (pf)
⊗ Decca 410 554-2 (modern alternative of the two most popular sonatas)

Opus 5   **Cello Sonatas Nos.1 & 2 in F major & G minor**
Opus 69   **Cello Sonata No.3 in A major**
Opus 102 **Cello Sonatas Nos.4 & 5 in C major & D major**

◆   Harrell (vc), Ashkenazy (pf)
  ⊗ Decca 417 628-2 (2)

WoO 45   Variations on Handel's 'See the Conquering
           Hero Comes'
WoO 46   Variations on Mozart's 'Bei Männern,
           welche Liebe'
Opus 66   Variations on Mozart's 'Ein Mädchen oder
           Weibchen'
◆   Ma (vc), Ax (pf)
  ⊗ CBS CD 42121

SOLO PIANO

Piano Sonatas Nos.1–32
◆   Kempff (pf)
  ⊗ DG 415 834-2

Opus 13   Piano Sonata No.8 in C minor, 'Pathétique'
Opus 27 No.1   Piano Sonata No.13 in E flat major
Opus 27 No.2   Piano Sonata No.14 in C sharp minor,
                'Moonlight'
◆   Gilels (pf)
  ⊗ DG 429 306-2

Opus 53   Piano Sonata No.21 in C major, 'Waldstein'
Opus 57   Piano Sonata No.23 in F minor, 'Appassionata'
Opus 81a   Piano Sonata No.26 in E flat major, 'Les Adieux'
◆   Gilels (pf)
  ⊗ DG 419 162-2

Opus 106   Piano Sonata No.29 in B flat major,
          'Hammerklavier'
◆   Gilels (pf)
  ⊗ DG 410 527-2

Opus 101   Piano Sonata No.28 in A major
Opus 106   Piano Sonata No.29 in B flat major,
          'Hammerklavier'
Opus 109   Piano Sonata No.30 in E major

Opus 110 **Piano Sonata No.31 in A flat major**
Opus 111 **Piano Sonata No.32 in C minor**
♦   Pollini (pf)
⊗ DG 419 199-2 (2)

Opus 90   **Piano Sonata No.27 in E minor**
Opus 101 **Piano Sonata No.28 in A major**
Opus 111 **Piano Sonata No.32 in C minor**
♦   Kovacevich (pf)
⊗ EMI CDC7 54599-2

Opus 34   **6 Variations in F major**
WoO 79   **5 Variations in D major on 'Rule, Britannia'**
WoO 70   **6 Variations in G major on Paisiello's 'Nel Cor Più non mi sento**
♦   Brendel (pf)
⊗ Philips 432 093-2 (c/w Schumann's *Etudes symphoniques*)

Opus 35   **15 Variations and a Fugue in E flat major, 'Eroica'**
♦   Gilels (pf)
⊗ DG 423 136-2

Opus 120 **33 Variations on a Waltz by Diabelli**
♦   Kovacevich (pf)
⊗ Philips 422 969-2

Opus 33   **7 Bagatelles**
Opus 119 **11 Bagatelles**
Opus 126 **6 Bagatelles**
♦   Kovacevich (pf)
⊗ Philips 426 976-2

WoO 59   **Bagatelle No.25 in A minor, 'Für Elise'**
Opus 51   **Rondos**
Opus 35   **Variations and Fugue in E flat major, 'Eroica'**
Opus 34   **6 Variations in F major**
♦   Lortie (pf)
⊗ Chandos CHAN 8616

Index

THE
CLASSIC *f*M
GUIDE TO
CLASSICAL MUSIC

JEREMY NICHOLAS
Consultant Editor: ROBIN RAY
Foreword by HUMPHREY BURTON

'*. . . a fascinating and accessible guide . . . it will provide
an informative and illuminating source of insight
for everybody from the beginner to the musicologist.*'

Sir Edward Heath

The Classic *f*M Guide to Classical Music opens with a masterly
history of classical music, illustrated with charts and lifelines, and
is followed by a comprehensive guide to more than 500 composers. There are major entries detailing the lives and works of the
world's most celebrated composers, as well as concise biographies
of more than 300 others.

This invaluable companion to classical music combines extensive factual detail with fascinating anecdotes, and an insight
into the historical and musical influences of the great composers.
It also contains reviews and recommendations of the best works,
and extensive cross-references to lesser-known composers.
Jeremy Nicholas's vibrant, informative and carefully researched
text is complemented by photographs and cartoons, and is designed for easy reference, with a comprehensive index.

£19.99   ISBN: 1 85793 760 0   **Hardback**
£9.99   ISBN: 1 86205 051 1   **Paperback**

CLASSIC *f*M

MUSIC

A JOY FOR LIFE

EDWARD HEATH

Foreword by Yehudi Menuhin

Music is a record of a lifetime's passion for a subject with which former Prime Minister Sir Edward Heath has been involved since he was nine years old. In this book – first published in 1976 and now updated in his eighty-first year – Sir Edward recalls his musical experiences, from his days as a chorister in his parish church to his work as a conductor of international renown – a career that began in 1971 when he conducted the London Symphony Orchestra playing Elgar's 'Cockaigne' Overture at its gala concert in the Royal Festival Hall.

From his friendships with Herbert von Karajan and Leonard Bernstein to his great musical loves such as Beethoven and British music, from music at Downing Street to a series of five symphony concerts he conducted for his eightieth birthday celebrations, Sir Edward gives a fascinating personal insight into his wide-ranging experience. Written with great knowledge and characteristic enthusiasm, *Music – A Joy for Life* will appeal both to those who already have a serious interest in music and also to those who enjoy music and would like a greater understanding.

£16.99 ISBN: **1 86205 090 2**

CLASSIC *f*M
LIFELINES

With 4.8 million listeners every week, *Classic fM* is now the most listened-to national commercial radio station in the UK. With the *Classic fM Lifelines*, Pavilion Books and *Classic fM* have created an affordable series of elegantly designed short biographies that will put everyone's favourite composers into focus.

Written with enthusiasm and in a highly accessible style, the *Classic fM Lifelines* series will become the Everyman of musical biographies. Titles for the series have been chosen from *Classic fM*'s own listener surveys of the most popular composers.

£4.99 each book

CLASSIC *f*M
LIFELINES

To purchase any of the books in the *Classic fM Lifelines* series
simply fill in the order form below and post or fax it,
together with your remittance, to the address below.

Please send the titles ticked below

J.S. Bach	☐	Gustav Mahler	☐
Ludwig van Beethoven	☐	Sergei Rachmaninov	☐
Johannes Brahms	☐	Franz Schubert	☐
Claude Debussy	☐	Dmitri Shostakovich	☐
Edward Elgar	☐	Pyotr Ilyich Tchaikovsky	☐
Joseph Haydn	☐	Ralph Vaughan Williams	☐

Number of titles @ £4.99 _____   Value: £_____
(carriage paid within UK)

I enclose a cheque (UK only) payable to Bookpoint ☐
OR
Please charge my credit card account ☐
I wish to pay by: Visa ☐ MasterCard ☐ Access ☐ American Express ☐

Card number ☐☐☐☐☐☐☐☐☐☐☐☐☐☐☐☐☐☐☐☐

Signature_____   Expiry Date_____
Name _____
Address _____
_____
_____   Postcode_____

Please send your order to: Marketing Department, Pavilion Books Ltd,
26 Upper Ground, London SE1 9PD, or fax for quick dispatch to:
Marketing Department, 0171-620 0042.